CW01669370

I absolutely love this book! I inte

20schemes for future elders, leaders, church planters and church revitalisers. The real beauty of the book lies in its easy accessibility for the average church member. This is a book every Christian ought to read and every church ought to study. Get on this cheeky little number right now!

~ Mez McConnell, Director of 20schemes,
Principal of The Ragged School of Theology

Many of the books I have read on eldership have been produced for those who are already familiar with church polity and are considering eldership. By contrast, this volume is easy to read yet comprehensive in describing the biblical case for eldership and independence. It is helpful to both mature believers thinking about church eldership and unchurched, first-generation Christians to learn about their responsibilities as church members.

~ Ian Williamson, Executive Director of Medhurst Ministries

Independent Eldership

by Stephen Kneale

GRACE PUBLICATIONS TRUST
62 Bride Street
London N7 8AZ
www.gracepublications.co.uk

First published in Great Britain by Grace Publications Trust 2026

©Stephen Kneale 2026

The right of Stephen Kneale to be identified as the author of this work has been asserted by him under the Copyright, Designs and Patents Act 1988. All rights reserved.

No part of this publication may be reproduced, stored in a retrieval system or transmitted in any form by any means, electronic, mechanical, photocopying, recording or otherwise, without the prior permission of the publisher or the Copyright Licensing Agency.

A record for this book is available from the British Library.

Unless otherwise noted, all Scripture quotations are taken from the Anglicised Christian Standard Bible®, Copyright © 2017 by Holman Bible Publishers. Used by permission. Christian Standard Bible® and CSB® is a federally registered trademark of Holman Bible Publishers.

Cover design by Pete Barnsley (CreativeHoot.com)

Printed in the UK by Ashford Colour Ltd.

ISBN Paperback: 978-1-917322-02-7
Ebook: 978-1-917322-03-4

Independent Eldership

by Stephen Kneale

Part of

'A PEOPLE ON PURPOSE'

Church Health Series

Grace
Publications

Contents

Introduction to the series 'A People on Purpose'

Healthy Christians make for healthy churches, and healthy churches make for healthy Christians. Likewise, healthy churches are led by healthy leaders who have been shaped by healthy resources.

This continuous loop is a momentum-filled space where discipleship and local church ministry take place, and its logic originates from God himself. Biblically ordered local churches are composed of Christians, of those who have placed saving faith in Christ alone for salvation and who have witnessed to this through believer's baptism. There literally is no such thing as 'the church' minus the redeemed people who make it up. The local church is the heart of gospel reality, the hub of Christian discipleship, and the unique hope that is in Christ made visible to a fallen world. We cannot hold too high a view of what the local church is, nor how important it is in God's sovereign purposes of redemption.

A People on Purpose is an original series of volumes with the health of the local church at its core. It is God who *gathers* his church, who ultimately *governs* his church, and who graciously *grows* his church in depth and breadth for his glory. These three realities form the framework for what this series seeks to address: providing biblically faithful teaching on what the church is, how its life can be ordered in line with Scripture, and how its growth can be fostered and cultivated, under God. The goal of the series is to encourage godly leadership, healthy congregationalism, and a church order which reflects the pattern and power found in the New Testament.

There is a great need for churches in the United Kingdom, Ireland, and further afield to set Christ-centred, Holy Spirit-dependent health at the heart of how they plant, revitalise, lead, preach, and plan their life together. While this series emerges from the context of British and Irish church life, it is our sincere prayer that churches in other parts of the world will benefit from it. Where references are made to cultural issues specific to the UK/Ireland, we have sought to provide explanations of their meaning, and extrapolation of the point to wider contexts. *A People on Purpose* is written by authors with experience in local church leadership in this specific context, and the whole series is designed to provide in-depth and practical teaching on the things that aid the healthy development of congregations. As such, these volumes are written for eldership teams and church memberships who are concerned to become better informed intellectually about what a healthy church looks like, and more fully conformed to this pattern in their week-by-week ministry.

Across ten volumes, the themes of *gather*, *govern*, and *grow* will be explored:

Gather: it is God who sovereignly gathers a people for himself. Three volumes of A *People on Purpose* will be devoted to how he does this and what this looks like practically in local church life. At the very foundation of church fellowships is the gospel itself, the good news of forgiveness of sins in Christ Jesus. In writing and thinking about the local church, it is all too easy to overlook what conversion is and why it is the bedrock of our life together. Similarly, the realities of baptism, membership and the Lord's Supper can feel like 'givens', obvious things that we do. Thinking through the biblical underpinnings of how the church is gathered can serve as a remedy for false thinking and a rescue from careless practice.

Govern: Christ Jesus is the Head of the church, and the early chapters of Revelation depict him as walking among the gritty details of local churches. The governance of Baptist churches should reflect the gloriously practical design that the Saviour himself has given, and the three volumes in this section examine eldership, congregationalism and church discipline. A biblically calibrated eldership, a gospel enriched congregationalism and a scripturally ordered form of discipline are crucial to the healthy life of every congregation. Exploring these features in detail can help to deliver local churches from the torpor of being under-led, the terror of being over-led, and the shame of being undisciplined. Handling these matters biblically, faithfully and sensitively can avoid many pitfalls for churches and their members, and can allow local churches to function effectively and winsomely in the world.

Grow: while good as far as it goes, a well-ordered body of people in possession of a strong sense of what the gospel is and how governance works does not make for a healthy church. The local church is not a dead gallery of good ideas, but a dynamic body of continuous growth. The three volumes in this section of *A People on Purpose* focus on how the local church engages in faithful mission (locally and globally), how discipleship can be developed and delivered in our life together, how mutual care should operate biblically, and how association between autonomous local churches can promote evangelism and mutual encouragement. Growth is often mistaken for numerical increase, but a model which aims for breadth rather than depth might be superficially successful but it cannot be scripturally faithful. Making true, biblical growth, part of how we think about our life together as a church is indispensable.

A final book in the series will provide chapter-length treatments of each theme, providing a resource that can be used for group and one-to-one study.

These books are offered to local churches with the prayer that the Saviour himself might use them to nurture greater esteem for the gospel, greater concern for biblical governance, and an increased burden for congregational growth. Healthy Christians make for healthy churches, and healthy churches make for healthy Christians. Likewise, healthy churches are led by healthy leaders who have been shaped by healthy resources.

May the Lord be glorified as we seek greater conformity to him in our individual lives and increased conformity to his pattern for what the local church is, and how it can function to the glory of his name.

Andrew Roycroft
Series Editor

Introduction to *Independent Eldership*

Discussions about church governance often meet with all the enthusiasm of a dental check-up. We know it matters in theory and may catch some problems but we're never going to enjoy it. Few ever followed Jesus because they fell in love with the church constitution or membership structures. It can all seem so unnecessary, a bit tiresome and likely to keep us away from all the important gospel matters that we want to be about.

The truth is, many people reckon church polity and governance just don't matter that much. That is, until something happens that requires a response. Then everybody wishes the constitution said something about what to do. That's the point at which everybody wishes there was some sort of process. Everybody wishes they knew who should do something and what, exactly, they are meant to do. If we ignore polity and governance, dismissing them as unimportant, we end up like those who wonder whether they should have taken gas safety regulations a bit more seriously after their boiler has blown up. These things never seem to matter - until they do! Something else always seems more important until it suddenly becomes the most pressing issue in front of us. Only, at that point, it's all too late. The processes and systems we need just aren't there and things start to fall apart.

The goal of the local church is not to be as efficient and organised as possible. Organisation and structures are means to an end, not the sum total of what we are aiming to do. The reason the church exists is to glorify God, enjoy him forever and equip God's people to do God's work. Local churches exist to grow believers to maturity in Christ and reach the lost with the gospel. They exist to do the work of discipleship and evangelism for God's glory. Structures and administration are not their primary focus, but that doesn't make them unimportant. Church structures and administration are secondary means of achieving the church's primary goals. Without them, the church will not fulfil its purpose to equip the saints and reach the lost to the glory of God.

Not only do organisation and administration matter, but the church that ignores Jesus' commands about how it should organise itself is not a healthy one. Tom Schreiner puts it this way:

> Jesus Christ is the head of the church, and we derive our instructions from him. The church is not a human institution or idea. The ordering of the church is not a matter of our wisdom or preference... He has given us instructions on the nature and design of the local church in His inspired and authoritative word. To jettison what

> God says about the church and supplant it with our own ideas is nothing less than astonishing arrogance.[1]

If this is true, we can't just wave away polity, structures and administration as though they don't matter. If we relegate everything that is not a gospel essential to the realm of secondary matters (for which read, unimportant), the Bible wouldn't need to be nearly so long. Why did God give us so much Scripture when a short gospel pamphlet would do? The Lord would only need to outline primary gospel matters and let us work out the rest of the trivial details for ourselves. But he didn't do that because, though these things do not determine our salvation, Jesus still thinks they're important. They may not be first order gospel issues but they are equally not indifferent matters. They matter enough for him to give instructions about them. If he went to the trouble of giving us these instructions about the church, he wants us to follow them. When all is said and done, we set aside what Jesus tells us to do at our own peril. That includes such secondary matters as church organisation, administration and structures.

But should we write these things off as unimportant as far as the gospel is concerned at any rate? When Paul wrote to Titus, his first concern was a matter of church polity. After a brief introduction, Titus 1:5 says, 'The reason I left you in Crete was to set right what was left undone and, as I directed you, to appoint elders in every town'. Paul then goes on to outline the qualifications for eldership. If this has nothing to do with the gospel, why is it Paul's first

---

1 Foreword to Merkle, B., 40 *Questions About Elders and Deacons*, Kregel Publications, 2008, p. 11

concern? Clifford Pond points out, 'we can be sure this was with a view to effective gospel outreach and we can also be sure the subject of good organisation did not occupy endless church time; in the long run good organisation saves time.'[2] This is supported by Acts 6 where the presenting issue in the Jerusalem church called for a structural solution. What is significant is that the specific fruit of that organisational restructuring was that 'the word of God spread, the disciples in Jerusalem increased greatly in number, and a large group of priests became obedient to the faith' (Acts 6:7). All of which is to say, healthy churches with healthy structures make healthy disciples who make healthy disciples. Establishing sound, biblical polity in our churches is an important means of achieving biblical gospel ends. Polity is, in the end, a gospel matter.

Some of the things that follow in this book may seem like common sense to some. If that is you, praise God that healthy church structures are clear in your mind. The problem, as they say, is that common sense is not so common. For many, these things are not at all obvious - indeed, they are deemed unimportant and frequently overlooked. The number of issues in churches that have come about because of failure to implement some of these biblical principles shows they are not clear to everyone. I make no apology for highlighting what some might consider obvious for the sake of the many who simply do not believe it is so.

I have started with biblical principles and then move on to practical application of those principles in the life of the local church. Churches exist in different contexts, they vary in size, finances and dozens of other things, but I trust that the biblical

---

2 Pond, C., *Only Servants*, Grace Publications Trust, 1991, p. 15

principles laid down here are rooted in the Scriptures, and that they can be applied in all churches in all places. I appreciate that some of the later practical application may not always apply to all churches everywhere. I have tried to be broad enough that even the practicalities may apply, or with minor tweaks become applicable, to most churches. Where they do not, and no specific biblical command or principle is cited, take it for what it is: one application of the key biblical principles by a fallible pastor to be taken or discarded as you see fit.

I have tried not to be too repetitive but appreciate some of the early principles need to be restated in later chapters. I have also purposefully tried to make each chapter stand in its own right. I hope you will see a flow of logic so that each chapter builds on what has come before. I do, necessarily, refer back to previous chapters at certain points.

Finally, let me highlight my indebtedness to Clifford Pond for his book *Only Servants*. I had initially hoped to see that book republished. For various reasons, that turned into a plan to write a new book on the same subject. But many of the principles outlined here overlap with *Only Servants* and it has played a significant part in forming my own understanding of biblical polity. Naturally, it is hardly a great a surprise that two Particular Baptists share some significant overlap on principles of polity! There are some key respects in which we differ, but where there is evident overlap, credit should be Clifford Pond's. In his introduction, he also cites a series of authors and says much the same as I am doing now. I trust that such a great cloud of witnesses suggests we are pushing in a biblical direction.

Chapter 1:

The Development of Independent Churches

Independent Churches have come about through a slow and gradual process of development and grew out of the English Puritanism of the sixteenth century, driven by a desire to follow the New Testament pattern for local church governance. We will explore the New Testament pattern for local churches in more detail in the next chapter, and there we will see that the New Testament churches believed each local congregation was directly responsible to Christ as head of the church and individually called to defend the gospel. Under the lordship of Jesus, they were to be guided by him in organising their own affairs, including the appointment of their leaders. But church history shows us that the New Testament pattern was soon abandoned.

By AD 112, Ignatius – the leader of the church in Antioch – was encouraging fellow believers to 'follow the bishop as Jesus

Christ followed the Father'.[1] The historian Mark Noll comments, 'His injunction revealed the emergence of a system of church organization [*sic*] constructed around locally powerful bishops who were assuming the tasks of guiding the faithful in their localities while deliberating with fellow bishops in other places about the general direction of the church.'[2]

By the end of the second century, Irenaeus – Bishop of Lyons – was arguing that bishops were the ones entrusted with guarding the Christian faith. He claimed an unbroken line of presiding bishops guaranteed the continuation of apostolic authority in the church. So, not only was Irenaeus arguing that bishops had greater authority than elders, but that they had the very authority of the Apostles.[3] By the middle of the third century, Cyprian – Bishop of Carthage – insisted this apostolic succession could be traced back to the Apostle Peter, arguing 'age has followed age and bishop has followed bishop in succession, and the office of the episcopate and the system of the Church has been handed down, so that the Church is founded on the bishops and every act of the Church is directed by those same presiding officers.'[4]

The early signs of these moves away from the New Testament pattern can be seen in the Bible. The Apostle John writes about a

1 As quoted in Noll, M., *Turning Points: Decisive Moments in the History of Christianity*, Inter-Varsity Press, 1997, p.31

2 Ibid., p.31

3 See ibid., p.40

4 As quoted in, ibid., p.40

particular elder,[5] 'I wrote something to the church, but Diotrephes, who loves to have first place among them, does not receive our authority' (3 Jn. 9). Here we have an elder seeking to place himself above the church and create a hierarchy within his eldership. Not only is he trying to make himself 'first', but he also places himself above the Apostles by rejecting their authority. This kind of desire for hierarchy, and particularly to be first in the church, laid the groundwork for the establishment of an episcopacy. In time, this would lead to the creation of the office of pope, with its doctrines of supreme authority and papal infallibility.

There have always been groups who protested against this tendency to impose centralised organisation and external structures on the local church. Clifford Pond notes that of those who attempted such reform from the second to the seventh centuries, 'most, if not all of them, embraced one or another kind of heresy, or eccentricity. But their aim was to restore a biblical order of churches composed of born again and, usually, baptised believers, independently responsible to Christ alone.'[6] After the establishment of Roman Catholic control over Western Europe from the seventh century, many continued to advocate for biblical

5 John Gill, in his Commentary on the Whole Bible, states 'it is very likely he was more than a private member in the church, and that he was an officer, and it may be the pastor... And it may be also, that he sought to have the pre-eminence over the rest of the elders of the church, for in those large churches there were oftentimes more elders and pastors than one; see Acts 20:17.' Similarly, The Pulpit Commentary states, 'That Diotrephes was bishop of this Church is conjecture ... He may have been an influential layman. But the context favours the view that he was at least a presbyter.'

6 Pond, *Only Servants*, p.20

change. Men such as Peter Waldo (twelfth century), John Wycliffe (fourteenth century) and Jan Huss (fifteenth century) amongst others all advocated for reform back to biblical, New Testament Christianity. By the sixteenth century, such calls for reform in Germany – led by Martin Luther – sparked the Protestant Reformation across Europe that caused new churches with biblical convictions to form outside of Roman Catholic structures.

In the years that followed, different groups came to various conclusions about where final authority lay in questions of teaching and leadership in the church. Mike Gilbart-Smith comments:

> Episcopalians argued that the church was to be overseen by bishops (the word used to translate the Greek word *episcopos*, literally 'overseer', in some Bible translations). The bishops themselves were to be answerable to the secular authority (particularly the monarch) in an established national church. Presbyterians argued that the office of elder (*presbuteros*) and overseer (*episcopos*) were one and the same, and the church was to be overseen by teaching elders who would gather from several local churches in presbyteries, and they themselves would meet with other presbyteries from other areas in synods to make decisions for the wider church in a nation, and hypothetically across the whole world. Essential to Presbyterianism is the idea that "many particular congregations may be under one church government." Independents agreed with Presbyterians on the unity of the offices of elder and bishop, but argued that elders were responsible only for

> the local church, and there were to be no presbyteries or synods with authority over local congregations. Like other Independents, Congregationalists argued for the independence of the local church, but added that within local churches, the elders themselves were answerable to the whole membership of the congregation, who were the final human authority in membership.[7]

In England, the established church became Anglican. They rejected the authority of the Pope and many doctrines of the Roman Catholic Church. However, they maintained rule by bishops and, after a brief flirtation with naming them Head of the Church, gave the role of supreme governor to the monarch. In Scotland, as in other parts of Europe, the state church became Presbyterian. Such churches later arrived in England. However, looking on at this new presbyterian polity, John Milton wrote in his poem 'On the New Forcers of Conscience Under the Long Parliament', 'new presbyter is but old priest writ large.'[8] Milton himself had previously abandoned his plan to be ordained in the Church of England because of what he considered to be the tyranny of the bishops.[9] For him, reform still fell short of what many perceived to be the New Testament model of independent, self-governing churches.

---

7 Gilbart-Smith, M., in Skull, D., King, A., Sayers, J., *Pure Church: Recovering God's Plan For Local Churches*, Grace Publications, 2022, p.193

8 Milton, John. (2007), *Selected Poems*, London: Penguin, 67

9 See Milton, J., The Reason of Church Government, Book 2, Accessed at: The John Milton Reading Room, https://milton.host.dartmouth.edu/reading_room/reason/book_2/text.shtml, accessed 02/09/2025

During the seventeenth century, Independents, Congregationalists and Baptists all sprang up, followed by Brethren congregations, arriving by the nineteenth century. Although there were differences in practice and theology, each of these churches believed it was right to be self-governing, and for the church to appoint its own leaders under the Lordship of Jesus without interference from outside parties or external structures. This remains the essence of modern independency today.

There are, of course, differences between independent churches. Some are baptistic, others are paedobaptist or dual practice. Some are Calvinistic in theology, others may be Amyraldian or Arminian. Some are congregational in their polity, others prefer to be elder-led. Some will call a pastor, others insist on elders alone. But they all have in common a belief in the independence of the local church to appoint its own leaders and not be ruled by any external structures or authorities.

Nevertheless, these differences do throw up questions. Is there a right and wrong way to operate as independent churches? Does the Bible have more to say beyond independently appointing our own leaders? We will turn to those questions shortly.

Chapter 2:

The Biblical Grounds for Independency

We finished the last chapter with a brief look at some of the differences between independent churches. Before we examine them in more detail, there is a more important issue to address. We have seen where Independents came from, but we haven't yet made the case for independency. It's important to see that the biblical case for independency is the ground on which other matters of church polity stand.

The basis for that claim is simple. New Testament churches existed even when they did not have elders to oversee them. Whilst we can see it was not the long-term plan, and we might argue it is not ultimately healthy to remain this way, it is nevertheless true that churches *existed* – and there was no question they were operating as *legitimate* churches – even though they had no elders (cf. Tit. 1:5; Acts 14:21–23). Mike Gilbart-Smith points out:

> Congregationalism is in fact *more* fundamental to the government of the local church than even the

> existence of elders in each church. Under the Holy Spirit the church is both competent to discern what a Christian is (through her understanding of the gospel) and who should be treated as a Christian (through the preservation and maintenance of a true doctrine and morality within the church). These responsibilities are given to the local church *as a whole* and may not be passed onto a smaller group within the church or those outside of the congregation. (emphasis original).[1]

The independence of the local church is clear in the New Testament. In Matthew 18:15–20 Jesus gives the responsibility of enacting church discipline to the local church. The steps for church discipline begin with one believer to another, then two or three as witnesses and, if the individual still does not repent, Matthew 18:17 says – clearest in the Tyndale Bible – 'If he heare not them tell it vnto the congregacion'. The King James Bible, which used the majority of Tyndale's translation, pointedly changed the word *congregation* to *church* in order to support external structures and maintain the position of the bishops and, most significantly, the King as supreme governor. King James I specifically commissioned his 1611 version in response to the perceived political problems with Tyndale's translation and some awkward notes in the Geneva Bible translation. The KJV text is largely the same as Tyndale's but for such political changes. Nevertheless, Tyndale's earlier translation makes clear it is the congregation who are to be told,

---

1 Gilbart-Smith, M. in *Pure Church*, p.194

not an external bishop. Church discipline is to be handled within the church and not through external structures.

Similarly, if we look at the setting apart of Paul and Barnabas for mission work in Acts 13:1–4, there are no external structures or bodies involved. We are told, 'As they were worshipping the Lord and fasting, the Holy Spirit said, "Set apart for me Barnabas and Saul for the work to which I have called them." Then after they had fasted, prayed, and laid hands on them, they sent them off.' The Holy Spirit led the church to set apart two men from within the congregation for mission work. No external authority was required.

Again, in 1 Corinthians 5, Paul writes to the church in Corinth concerning a man who is sleeping with his father's wife. The whole chapter amounts to Paul encouraging the church to enact meaningful discipline. But Paul insists in 1 Corinthians 5:2 that the church should have already removed this person from membership. Paul is writing to them to encourage them to do what they already should have done and have the power and authority amongst themselves to do. The church in Corinth did not need special permission from any external body to defend the gospel and enact proper church discipline.

In 2 Thessalonians 3:6 Paul says, 'we command you, brothers and sisters, in the name of our Lord Jesus Christ, to keep away from every brother or sister who is idle and does not live according to the tradition received from us.' Here, the local church is told that they are responsible for guarding the traditions passed on to them by the Apostles. Contrary to the claims of Irenaeus and Cyprian that we read in the first chapter, the apostolic faith and traditions are to be maintained and defended by each local church.

Defence of the gospel and the apostolic tradition is given to local congregations. This is the same in 1 John 4:1. The local church to whom John is writing is told 'do not believe every spirit, but test the spirits to see if they are from God, because many false prophets have gone out into the world.' Defence of the gospel, right teaching of the word, maintaining the apostolic tradition and holding to the faith once for all delivered to the saints is given by the Apostles to local churches. These commands and instructions are not given to external authorities or parties of any kind, but to local congregations of believers.

We also see this in the letters to the seven churches in Revelation 2 and 3. These local churches are told to ensure false prophets do not creep in amongst them. It is worth noticing that the threat of lampstands being removed is not one of overseers, bishops and synods removing congregations from their denominational structures, but rather the Lord Jesus directly determining whether this local congregation remains a true church or not. Each of these local churches is not responsible to a bishop, but rather under the Lordship and Headship of Christ they are seen to be individual, independent congregations. For this reason, Jesus addresses each of the churches directly.

Throughout the New Testament, we see self-governing, local churches responsible for their own affairs and answerable ultimately to Jesus. They handled matters of administration, church discipline, ministry, and evangelism themselves. The letters of the New Testament are written to local churches that were expected to organise themselves and respond to apostolic instruction as a congregation. The only external authority we see is that of the Apostles.

At this point, someone might argue that the Apostles themselves give grounds for external authority. Indeed, we have already seen the likes of Irenaeus and Cyprian argue that apostolic authority continues to be passed down through bishops. Some will point to the so-called Jerusalem council in defence of external authority. They may also highlight Paul and Barnabas appointing elders in churches in Acts 14 and the instruction for Titus to 'appoint elders in every town' (Tit. 1:5) as evidence that the early churches were not self-governing in the way we have described above.

The reason I refer to the 'so-called' Jerusalem Council is that it was not really a council in any meaningful sense at all. The meeting in Acts 15 was not a representative meeting of all the regional churches, but a specific meeting between two local churches. The only churches explicitly involved were from Jerusalem and Antioch, and there is no reason to believe any other churches were part of the discussion. Some note that Paul and Barnabas passed through Phoenicia and Samaria on their way to Jerusalem, but Benjamin Merkle points out: 'There is no mention that the churches in Phoenicia and Samaria sent representatives along with Paul and Barnabas to Jerusalem. After the decree was written, it was to be sent, not only to the church in Antioch, but also the churches in Syria and Cilicia. Again, nowhere do we read that churches from these regions participated in the proceedings.'[2]

Further, the meeting between the two churches was not initiated by the 'mother church' in Jerusalem. Rather, Acts 15:1–2

---

2 Merkle, *40 Questions*, p.33

gives us two important details. First, 'some men came down from Judea' arguing that circumcision was necessary for salvation. The false gospel that was being spread had come from the region of Jerusalem. So, the reason for the meeting between the two churches was that an issue appeared to have arisen in one of the churches and was now being exported to another. Second, 'After Paul and Barnabas had engaged them in serious argument and debate, Paul and Barnabas and some others were appointed to go up to the apostles and elders in Jerusalem about this issue.' The meeting was not called by the church in Jerusalem, but initiated by the church in Antioch. The church in Antioch was not summoned by the 'mother church', rather those in Antioch initiated a meeting with the church in Jerusalem, as an independent church, to clarify the issues that came from Judea.

We should also note that this was not an ordinary meeting of church leaders. Louis Berkhof – a Presbyterian who believed in external structures – acknowledges this when he says, 'this council was composed of apostles and elders, and therefore did not constitute a proper example and pattern of a classis or synod in the modern sense of the word.'[3] At this point in time, the Apostles were still involved in helping the church and its elders find their feet. They took a leading role in the meeting and are mentioned first each of the five times 'the apostles and elders' are referred to in Acts 15. As there are no apostles around today, this is not a repeatable meeting.

Perhaps most notably of all, the decree that is sent to the churches includes non-binding decisions. Robert Stein writes:

---

3 Berkhof, L., *Systematic Theology*, Banner of Truth Trust, 1988, p.591

> The issue at stake, according to Luke, is not justification but rather social intercourse between Jews and Gentiles. The decree does not add a requirement for Gentiles who are seeking salvation. Rather they are directions given by the Spirit (Acts 15:28) which seek to promote sensitivity on the part of Gentile Christians with respect to issues that were especially sensitive to the Jews.[4]

Though the issue (of circumcision being required for salvation) needed to be dealt with in a clear way, at least three of the four additional prohibitions were non-binding pleas for sensitivity.[5] As Darrell Bock puts it, 'the list is not so much about the law as having a spirit of sensitivity about that which may cause offense... There is a cultural sensitivity here where the issue is not establishing a fixed set of practices but respecting the practices of others and not forcing oneself on another because of such views.'[6] Benjamin Merkle summarises: 'the decision made by the council that the Gentiles needed to avoid certain foods is best understood, not as a binding decree set by an ecclesiastical authority, but as a plea for

---

4 'Jerusalem' in Hawthorne, G.F., Martin, R.P. and Reid, D.G. (Eds.), *Dictionary of Paul and His Letters*, Inter-Varsity Press, Leicester, 1993, p.471

5 Even the prohibition on refraining from sexual immorality – which clearly is binding – might well be best understood in the context of ritual laws. Darrell Bock comments: 'It is quite likely that the prohibition relates especially to attending pagan temples and what goes with them' in *Baker Exegetical Commentary on the New Testament*: Acts, Baker Publishing, Grand Rapids, 2007, p.506

6 Bock, Acts, p.507

sensitivity to the Jewish people.[7] For these reasons, the so-called Jerusalem Council does not provide a compelling basis for external structures and hierarchical church polity.

Neither should we see Paul and Barnabas appointing elders in Acts 14:23, nor similarly Paul's instruction in Titus 1:5, as an external authority imposing elders on local churches. Two examples of appointments happen earlier in Acts and set the pattern for the appointment of leaders. These come in Acts 1 – at the appointment of Matthias – and Acts 6, when the seven are chosen to serve.

In Acts 1:15, we're told that Peter stood up in front of the 120 members of the Jerusalem Church and explained the need for a replacement Apostle to return their number to twelve following the betrayal and death of Judas Iscariot. Having explained his rationale, Peter gives the qualifications for appointing this new Apostle (1:21–22). We then read in vv23–26:

> So they proposed two: Joseph, called Barsabbas, who was also known as Justus, and Matthias. Then they prayed, "You, Lord, know everyone's hearts; show which of these two you have chosen to take the place in this apostolic ministry that Judas left to go where he belongs." Then they cast lots for them, and the lot fell to Matthias and he was added to the eleven apostles.

Note the repeated use of the word *they*. Peter did not elect or appoint this Apostle himself. At no point in the passage are the Apostles distinguished from the rest of the 120 gathered together.

---

7 Merkle, 40 *questions*, p.36

There is no reason to assume that *they* refers exclusively to the Apostles here, and it certainly can't mean just Peter in the singular. This leaves us to conclude that the 120 proposed the two men, the whole congregation then prayed together about it and, through the casting of lots (the last time we read of this as a decision-making tool in the New Testament), the congregation elected Matthias. So, the first leadership appointment we read about in Acts was not imposed on the church by the Apostles, but was a collective decision of the whole congregation in Jerusalem.

In Acts 6:1–7, we see something similar in the appointment of the seven chosen to serve. A complaint about the distribution of food arose, and we read in vv2–3 'The Twelve summoned the whole company of the disciples and said, "It would not be right for us to give up preaching the word of God to wait on tables. Brothers and sisters, select from among you seven men of good reputation, full of the Spirit and wisdom, whom we can appoint to this duty."' So, again, we see the whole church gathered together and, this time articulated even more clearly, the Apostles ask the congregation to select seven men to serve. The matter moved forward because, v5 tells us, 'This proposal pleased the whole company.' Once the church had selected the seven men, the Apostles appointed them to serve by praying and laying hands on them. F.F. Bruce says, 'it was the community as a whole that selected these seven men and presented them to the apostles for their approbation; it was the apostles who installed them in office. This they did by laying their hands on them, after prayer.'[8] David Peterson notes, 'this should

8 Bruce, F.F., *The New International Commentary On The New Testament: The Book of Acts*, Eerdmans Publishing, Grand Rapids, 1988, p.122

not be understood in terms of postbiblical ideas of ordination'[9] and Darrell Bock agrees that 'the laying on of hands is strictly symbolic; formal ordination into ministry is a later practice of the church.'[10] In this way, the church community as a whole appointed the seven.

This pattern, established twice in the early chapters of Acts, is significant when it comes to understanding Acts 14:23 and Titus 1:5. It's often assumed that Paul and Barnabas chose leaders for the churches in Galatia and then appointed them as elders. This assumption then leads to the inference that Paul and Barnabas – and later Titus and Timothy – are effectively acting as episcopal bishops here. However, based on the pattern established in Acts 1 and Acts 6 for church appointments, it seems more likely that the phrase 'appointed elders' in Acts 14:23 and the instruction to 'appoint elders' in Titus 1:5 are shorthand for the process outlined in Acts 1 and 6. This is supported by Paul's instruction to Timothy not to be 'too quick to appoint anyone as an elder' (1 Tim. 5:22). These congregations chose men from among themselves and then Paul and Barnabas – and similarly Titus and Timothy – 'appointed' these men, that is: they publicly recognised the church's choice through the laying on of hands. The appointment of elders in the local church is a matter for the local church congregation.

Clearly, there was an external authority vested in the Apostles themselves. But two things are worth saying. First, as Clifford Pond points out:

---

9 Peterson, D., *The Pillar New Testament Commentary: The Acts of the Apostles*, Eerdmans Publishing, Grand Rapids, 2009, p.235

10 Bock, Acts, p.262

> There was only one external authority, namely, the Apostles. But even those apostles directed the local churches to deal with their own problems (1 Corinthians 5; Philippians 2:12–13). They did not tell them to wait for an apostle to be present in order to exercise direct authority, nor did they refer them to any other church authority, indeed they urged the churches to act themselves.[11]

Notably, the churches in Revelation 2 and 3 are likewise not directed to any external authorities, not even that of the Apostle John writing the letter, but are addressed directly by the Lord Jesus and assumed to have all that they need within the congregation to act on his instructions to them.

Second, it is clear that Apostles and elders occupy different roles. Whatever else is going on in Acts 15, we can see two distinct groups: Apostles and elders. The Apostles exercised some external authority over the congregations, but elders were responsible for particular local churches. This is significant because the role of apostle ended with the death of John, the last of the Apostles to die. The only people who ever exercised external authority over local churches were Apostles, and by the second century, there were no more Apostles. If there are no more Apostles, there can be no legitimate external oversight of the church. There is no apostolic authority because there is no longer an apostolic function. There is no call for external oversight to defend the gospel once for all delivered to the saints because, as we have seen already, that

---

11 Pond, *Only Servants*, p.23

task has been entrusted to the local church. The authority of the Apostles over all the churches has now been finally enshrined in the New Testament writings. They left elders to have oversight of local churches, and instituted no external structures or authorities to come after them. Indeed, as Clifford Pond notes in relation to the churches in Revelation:

> Each church is addressed separately and each church is required to apply the Lord's instructions under its own leadership. Enough time had elapsed after Pentecost for some synodical or other church structure to be advocated, or a 'bishop' to be appointed; but this was not the Lord's plan for the churches. Each was responsible to him directly.[12]

The local church, then, is to be independent. It is to be answerable directly to Jesus as its head. Local churches are to be free from external authorities and structures as self-governing, independent entities.

Of course, none of that means local churches have nothing to do with one another. Independent churches are interdependent. Local churches are still called to cooperate together for the sake of the gospel. So, it is to this we will turn next.

12 Ibid., p.24

Chapter 3:

Independency and Interdependence

One of the accusations thrown at independency is that of isolationism. Sadly, there is a streak of separatism that often rears its head and an underlying Elijah-complex that wants to insist 'we're the only ones left' or 'we are the only true church'. Just as Elijah was wrong about that, so are the churches that operate in this way. Being fiercely independent can lead some to foolish isolation. But the New Testament calls churches to show their unity together in Christ by practical interdependence without trading away their independence.

We have already seen the pattern of self-governing independency in the New Testament churches, but we also see local independent churches working together interdependently. In Acts 11:20–24, when some Cypriot and Cyrenian believers went to Antioch and people began trusting the Lord, the Jerusalem church heard about it and sent Barnabas to encourage and build up the fledgling church. By the end of Acts 11, we see the church in Antioch return the favour by sending famine relief to the believers in Jerusalem, sending it with Saul and Barnabas and giving it to the elders to distribute according to need.

In Acts 16:1–3 we see that the church in Lystra sent Timothy to go on mission with the Apostle Paul. This was a local church sending a missionary to reach unevangelised areas of the world. By Acts 20, there are various churches sending missionaries to help Paul. Acts 20:4 says, 'He was accompanied by Sopater son of Pyrrhus from Berea, Aristarchus and Secundus from Thessalonica, Gaius from Derbe, Timothy, and Tychicus and Trophimus from the province of Asia.' All these places, at this point, had established churches in them. Each of these men represents a local church sending their people out on mission for the sake of the gospel. Yet these men from separate churches all come together to cooperate in the work of mission.

Nevertheless, none of these things compromise the independence of the local church. Sending missionaries from a church to work alongside people from other churches is a matter for the local church themselves. Each local church decides who to send, where to send and how to send. Independency means no external structure or authority can compel a particular local church to send its people anywhere. But when individual churches determine to send people on mission for the sake of the gospel, this is their own autonomous choice. When various independent churches agree to send people from their respective churches out on mission together, these remain independent, autonomous choices of individual churches. Such collaborative efforts exemplify churches independently choosing to cooperate together for the cause of the gospel.

Not only do churches send people, but we also see local churches supporting the ministry of the gospel financially. In Philippians 4:14–16, Paul says 'you did well by partnering with me in my hardship. And you Philippians know that in the early days of the gospel, when I left Macedonia, no church shared with me in the matter of giving and receiving except you alone. For even in Thessalonica you sent gifts for my need several times.' Here is a church being thanked by Paul for financially supporting him in his ministry. Local, independent churches may support the work of missionaries financially, even when they have not sent the workers themselves.

We also see Paul encouraging wealthier churches to support ongoing ministry within poorer congregations. In 2 Corinthians 8 and 9, Paul encourages the church in Corinth to support the poorer Jerusalem church. Again, sending financial support and gifts for the sake of the gospel did not compromise the independence of these churches. Even with the legitimate authority of an Apostle, Paul did not compel the church in Corinth to give, but encouraged each individual to 'do as he has decided in his heart – not reluctantly or out of compulsion, since God loves a cheerful giver.' (2 Cor. 9:7) Indeed, they had already promised to give (cf. 2 Cor. 9:5). Paul spends the first part of chapter 9 explaining that he has been boasting about their generosity and it has encouraged others to be similarly generous. But he doesn't want the Corinthians to be unprepared and for it to look like he was blowing hot air; that would be shameful for everyone. The point is that even Paul with his apostolic authority does not compel or command the Corinthians to give. Their giving doesn't undermine their independency because it is their own autonomous choice to support gospel ministry. This decision has not been imposed on them by external pressure, not even by an Apostle who (one might assume) has the authority to do so.

In the previous chapter, we looked at the meeting between the churches in Jerusalem and Antioch. The aim of the meeting was to work out what to do about men from Judea who were exporting a false gospel to another region. Nevertheless, the cooperation between the two churches meant that core gospel issues were reaffirmed and some lesser cultural issues were ironed out between Jewish and Gentile believers. Neither church was binding the other, but their cooperation led to a strengthening of gospel values and a better understanding of their respective cultures.

There is evidence of associationism in the New Testament, too. Frequently, the Bible speaks of the churches together in a particular place. For example, we read about 'the churches of Galatia' (Gal. 1:2; 1 Cor. 16:1), 'the churches of Asia' (1 Cor. 16:19, Rev. 1:4,11) and the 'Judean churches' (Gal. 1:22). The use of the plural *churches* implies that these are groups of independent churches in a particular geographical region. Nevertheless, that the Apostle Paul can write to them together suggests a level of mutual involvement with one another. Kenneth Good argues that this 'leads us to believe that there was an early practice of fellowshipping together in common causes to a degree which would allow for mutual cooperation without the surrender of local autonomy.'[1]

So, we have seen some of the ways local churches supported one another: they sent people and workers to encourage the churches,

---

1 Good, K., *God's Blueprint For A Church: A Study Of Baptist Distinctive*, Backus Book Publishers, Rochester, New York, 1987, p.114

they sent missionaries for gospel work in unevangelised areas, and they sent financial support to more needy congregations. This fellowship and cooperation between local churches allowed them to accomplish things for the cause of the gospel that would not easily happen through a single church. Independency does not mean isolation, and local church autonomy does not rule out inter-church cooperation.

Today, independent churches may join associations, conventions or gospel partnerships. Groups such as the Fellowship of Independent Evangelical Churches (FIEC), the Grace Baptist Associations or one of the regional Gospel Partnerships all serve to bring churches together for the sake of the gospel. Joining such groups does not undermine the independency of the local church because these organisations do not have the authority to compel local churches to act one way or another. Gospel partnerships can decide they do not want to affiliate with a particular local church, they can decide to withdraw fellowship from a local church, but what they cannot do is compel a local church to do what that body of believers does not want to do or believe to be right.

Any external body that is seeking the authority to determine what a church may do – and the power to enforce such things – is not seeking to be a gospel partnership of independent churches, but a denomination that holds hierarchical power. Such denominationalism is not represented anywhere in the pages of Scripture. Kenneth Good notes:

> That there was a common life and experience in which the early churches shared is evident from the reading of the New Testament. That there was mutual fellowship

> is readily deduced from the notations on the reciprocal sense of love, mutual concern, and a common faith. But there is no revelation of any organizational [*sic*] structure which busied itself with the details of these concerns. Nothing beyond the local church appears in the record insofar as ecclesiastical machinery is concerned.[2]

Denominationalism does not exist in the biblical text, but independent churches deciding to associate together is not only a credible expression of independency, but a biblical approach to gospel unity and true catholicity.

If we are not called to place particular men or denominational structures over the church, what does the Bible say about authority in the church? Who has supreme authority, who governs the church and does it really matter? This is what we'll think about next.

2 Ibid., p.114

Chapter 4:

The Ultimate Rule of Christ Through Scripture

In the first chapter, we noted that in the years following the Protestant Reformation many churches disagreed over where authority lay in the church. However, two points of agreement existed across Protestant churches. First, Jesus Christ is Head of the Church. Second, the Bible, as the word of God, is the final authority in matters of faith and practice.

The Church of England initially established Henry VIII – the ruling monarch at the time of its creation – as Supreme Head of the Church by passing the 1536 Act of Supremacy. His Catholic daughter, Mary I, repealed the Act of Supremacy in 1555 in an attempt to bring the English Church back under the authority of the Pope. When Elizabeth I ascended to the throne, she passed the Act of Supremacy 1558 restoring authority back to the monarch. However, the role established by Henry VIII was changed to

Supreme Governor of the Church of England in recognition that only Christ can lay claim to be Head of the Church.

Since then, there has been a consensus among Protestant Churches that Jesus alone is Head. Louis Berkhof writes:

> The Reformation was a reaction against the externalism of Rome in general, and in particular, also against its external conception of the Church. It brought the truth to the foreground once more that the essence of the Church is not found in the external organisation of the Church, but in the Church as the *communio sanctorum* [communion of saints]. For both [Martin] Luther and [John] Calvin the Church was simply the community of the saints, that is, the community of those who believe and are sanctified in Christ, and who are joined to Him as their Head. This is also the position taken in the Reformed confessional standards.[1]

Scripturally, the point is beyond doubt. Jesus announces, after his resurrection, that 'All authority has been given to me in heaven and on earth' (Mt. 28:18) and Ephesians 1:22 similarly tells us that God has 'subjected everything under his feet and appointed him as head over everything.' Such supreme authority over all things must include the church. But we don't have to settle for logical inferences like that because in Colossians 1:18 we are told explicitly: Jesus 'is also the head of the body, the church.'

1 Berkhof, *Systematic Theology*, p.564

The mistake of the newly-formed Church of England was seeking to establish a Head of the Church despite the fact that God had already appointed one. No church, organisation or committee can appoint a Head of the Church. God has determined that only one man will have authority over his churches. As Clifford Pond puts it, 'He has set his dear Son in the seat of power and he has not delegated that authority to anyone else. Christ alone must rule the kingdom and each local church (Revelation 1:12–20).'[2] It is vital for churches to understand this. The Bible says Jesus is the 'chief Shepherd' (1 Pet. 5:4) and all other roles in the church act under the supreme authority of Christ.

The other point of agreement amongst Protestant churches is that the Bible is their final authority in matters of faith and practice. That is to say, Scripture is the final authority for the church. This was really the key issue of the Reformation. R.C. Sproul says, 'Historians have frequently explained the Protestant Reformation by describing its material cause and its formal cause. Its material cause was the dispute over the doctrine of justification by faith alone (*sola fide*); its formal cause, the dispute over biblical authority (*sola Scriptura*). The principle of *sola Scriptura* lurked in the background throughout the debate over justification.'[3] Although Protestant churches recognise other forms of authority, all of them are subordinate to the authority of God as revealed in the Scriptures and none of them can be ultimate because they are all capable of error. John Benton puts it this way:

---

2 Pond, *Only Servants*, p.29

3 Sproul, R.C., *What Is Reformed Theology: Understanding The Basics*, Baker Books, Grand Rapids, USA, 2016, p.50

> The great glory of the church is that it is the Lord's church. Even the smallest group of the Lord's people, who with a biblical discipline meet regularly together to encourage one another and evangelise the district, belong to the Lord. The church is his property. He is the head. He is the owner. Not the pastor. Not the elders. Not even the people themselves. We are not our own. We have been bought at the great price of Christ's blood.[4]

If Jesus is Head of the Church, and churches are directly responsible to the Lord Jesus, then we need some way to understand what it is that he requires of his people. God has revealed himself fully in the person of Jesus, but how has Jesus made himself known to us? The answer is through Scripture. The doctrine of Scripture alone and the belief that Jesus is Head of the Church necessarily hang together. We know what the Head *of* the Church wants *for* the church by reading what his word says *about* the church. The authority that Jesus gives to the church is made known through Scripture. That is why Benjamin Merkle says all pastors and elders 'shepherd God's flock under the authority of Jesus and his word. The authority of any church leader is always a derived authority. Jesus administrates His church by means of the word and the Spirit, and all human leaders are subject to these.'[5]

The Bible presents Jesus as the head of a body in which believers in the local church are members (cf. Eph. 1:22–23, 4:15–16; Col. 1:18).

---

4 Benton, J., *The Big Picture for Small Churches*, EP Books, Darlington, UK, 2020, p.180

5 Merkle, *40 Questions*, p.30

Whatever else we make of this body imagery, it implies a close connectedness between Jesus and his church. Jesus describes himself as a vine and his people as the branches (Jn. 15:1–8), again implying a close connectedness between Christ and his people. Just as our heads determine what the limbs in our bodies do, so Jesus as Head of the Church determines exactly what the members of his church do. The headship of Christ is meaningless if it doesn't mean that the church is to submit to his rule and authority through the Scriptures.

Nevertheless, if Jesus really is Head of the Church, there will be some clear signs of his rule. If the church is closely connected to Christ, what would we expect to see in practice? At least six things follow.

First, we would expect to see a meaningful focus on the word of God. If Jesus is Head of the Church, and he exercises his authority through the word, a church that recognises him as Head is going to have a strong focus on the Bible. If the word is central to Christ's rule, we would expect churches to be constantly in the Scriptures seeking out what Jesus has to say. In practice, this is likely to be seen in regular preaching of the word and Bible studies, but it will also be seen whenever discipleship is taking place or the church is thinking through a particular issue. Everything will ultimately be brought under the rule of Christ by submitting to the final authority of his word in all things.

Second, the church will be prayerful. As we look into the word, we see the church is called to be 'persistent in prayer' (Rom. 12:12) and to 'pray constantly' (1 The. 5:17). The Puritan writer, John Bunyan, says 'the people of the Lord in all humility are to lay themselves and their prayers, and all they have, at the foot of their God, to be disposed of by him as he in his heavenly wisdom sees best.'[6] In other words, if Jesus really is Head of the Church, his people are going to approach him in prayer and seek to align their will with his; what they want to do will mirror what he would have them do.

Third, there will be a desire to pursue holiness. 1 Peter 1:15–16 says, 'as the one who called you is holy, you also are to be holy in all your conduct; for it is written, **Be holy, because I am holy**.' Paul tells us in Romans 8:29 that Christians have been chosen by God to be 'conformed to the image of his Son'. God has called us to become more like Jesus. That is what Paul means in Ephesians 4:15 when he says 'let us grow in every way into him who is the head – Christ.' If Jesus is the Head of the Church, we will be growing more and more like him in the holiness to which he calls us.

Fourth, there will be love for the church. Jesus gave the world a measure of whether we are truly following him. John 13:34–35 says, '"I give you a new command: Love one another. Just as I have loved you, you are also to love one another. By this everyone will know that you are my disciples, if you love one another."' If the church is not characterised by a love for Jesus' people, it is a sign that they are not true disciples. A church with Christ as its Head will be a church that loves God's people. As the Apostle John said in his letter, 'If anyone says, "I love God," and yet hates his brother or sister, he is a liar. For the person who does not love his brother or sister whom he has seen cannot love God whom he has not seen. And we have this command from him: The one who loves God must also love his brother and sister' (1 Jn. 4:20–21).

---

6 Bunyan, J., *Prayer*, The Banner of Truth Trust, Edinburgh, UK, 1965, p.22

Fifth, the church with Christ as its Head will have unity among its members. In Ephesians 4:1–16, Paul is at pains to point out the unity that should characterise the Church of God. Unity is a clear consequence of Jesus being the Head of the Church. As Paul writes: 'There is one body and one Spirit – just as you were called to one hope at your calling – one Lord, one faith, one baptism, one God and Father of all, who is above all and through all and in all' (Eph. 4:4–6). If we are all subject to the same Head, and all recognise the authority of the same Scriptures, there will be an evident unity among people all working to the same end under the same Lord.

Sixth, if Jesus is Head of the Church, there will be a balance between order through structure and freedom of movement. The Head of a body gives direction and instruction, yet each member still has its own tasks to do. In a body there is structure and interconnectedness without denying the reality that hands and ears cannot do what eyes and feet are designed for and *vice versa*. As Paul clearly expounds in 1 Corinthians 12:21–27: we all rely on one another, we are all connected, and yet we are all different. This means there will be structure within the local church that allows each part of the body to be connected properly and work together cooperatively, but there will also be enough freedom to allow each part to do what it is designed to do. The church with Christ as its head will be characterised by an interconnected unity that allows each individual part of the body to operate properly, independently and yet in harmony with the whole. There will be enough organisation to ensure the body is a coordinated unit, whilst not being so overbearing that each part of the body cannot move freely as it ought.

If Jesus is the Head of the Church, it bears asking how the rest of the body ought to be organised? How does Jesus exercise his headship in the local church in practice? The next chapter will explore this more fully.

Chapter 5:

The Subordinate Rule of the Members

We have seen that each local church is directly responsible to the Lord Jesus Christ as Head of the Church. This necessarily means there is no external authority that can direct the local church from outside. So how should local churches be structured internally?

Amongst independents, there is no straightforward agreement. You will find those who believe in rule by elders, with church leaders appointing new elders without congregational involvement. Others argue for a similar position whilst also insisting upon a 'first amongst equals' model which, in effect, gives a pastor a higher level of authority than other elders. Some dispense with elders altogether and insist on a single pastor overseeing the church – sometimes calling this man a bishop – with a diaconal board operating underneath him to carry out his spiritual vision. All these approaches can rightly be characterised as independent since they do not have any external structures or outside individuals exercising authority over them.

However, the Bible outlines three key areas of responsibility that belong to the church body as a whole. The nature of these areas of responsibility shows us that the highest authority within the local church, operating under the headship of Christ, is the congregation. It is true that the church is also called to appoint elders and we may have questions about how they can meaningfully lead a church when their authority is under the membership they are called to serve. We will address those questions in later chapters. At this point, however, we are going to see that under the headship of Christ, it is the members that rule the church.

Before we look at these three areas of congregational rule, let's note the theological ground that underpins it. We have already seen that the formal cause of the Reformation was a fundamental disagreement about where authority lies in the church: is the church bound by Scripture alone or are there two infallible sources of authority for the church, the Bible and the Pope? The Reformers insisted that Scripture alone was the final source of authority in matters of faith and practice. From that core belief flowed other important convictions concerning the church.

By insisting on the doctrine of Scripture alone, Martin Luther was in turn led to the view there was no distinction between the clergy and laity – between the ordained leaders of the church and its ordinary members. He not only rejected the Pope, but the entire priesthood. Bruce Milne says, 'He restored the idea of the church as a spiritual communion of believers, all of whom are priests to God'.[1] This doctrine of the priesthood of all believers was developed from

1 Milne, B., *Know The Truth*, Inter-Varsity Press, Leicester, England, 1982, p.245

the explicit statements of 1 Peter 2:5,9 and Revelation 1:6 which refer to all believers as 'a holy priesthood', 'a royal priesthood' and such like. Peter also refers to believers offering 'spiritual sacrifices' as priests. Hebrews 13:15–16 and Romans 12:1–2 likewise speak about believers offering sacrifices of praise and presenting our bodies as living sacrifices, putting each believer in the role of a priest bringing offerings and sacrifices directly to God. Jonathan Leeman says:

> The universality of this priesthood, at least for early Luther, meant that church power rests in the whole congregation. The church possessed the authority to name officers:
>
> > For whoever comes out of the water of baptism can boast that he is already consecrated priest, bishop and pope, though ... just because we are all in like manner priests, no one must put himself forward and undertake, without our consent and election, to do what is in the power of all of us. For what is common to all, no one dare take upon himself without the will and the command of the community.
>
> The universal priesthood also meant any believer could baptize in a pinch: "In cases of necessity any one [*sic*] can baptize and give absolution, which would be impossible unless we were all priests." Or interpret Scripture: "An ordinary man may have true understanding; why then should we not follow him" against any errors of popes or bishops? Or reprove the pope or any erring Christian:

> "But if I am to accuse him before the Church, I must bring the Church together."[2]

It is this theology of the priesthood of all believers that underpins the authority God has given the congregation to rule in the local church. More specifically, the Bible teaches that the church community is given the authority to determine: who belongs, what is taught and who can lead.

Who belongs

In Matthew 18:15–20, Jesus outlines the steps of church discipline in matters of private sin. In the third and final step – if a person still refuses to repent – Jesus says the matter is to be told to the church. If the person does not listen to the church, the congregation is to treat them like a Gentile or tax collector. Mike Gilbart-Smith notes, 'Jesus doesn't say, "Tell it to the elders", "Tell it to the bishop", or "Tell it to the pastor", but "Tell it to the church" ... [He] insists that the church herself must speak with one voice to the errant brother or sister, and that only the church may ultimately take the step of removing them from visible covenant membership.'[3]

Only the congregation can legitimately remove a person from the church. In 1 Corinthians 5 – outlining a case of serious public sin – even Paul, with his apostolic authority, didn't reckon he had the right to expel the person in question from the church. He says in vv4–5, 'When you are assembled in the name of our Lord Jesus

---

2 Leeman, J., 'A Baptist View on The Royal Priesthood Of All Believers', *Southern Baptist Journal of Theology*, 23.1, Spring 2019, p.123

3 Gilbart-Smith, M., *Pure Church*, p.196

... hand that one over to Satan for the destruction of the flesh'. Paul could not remove this person from membership himself but insists the church must gather together and only then can they 'hand that one over to Satan', that is to remove him from the church. Gilbart-Smith writes, 'the apostle Paul, even as an apostle, could not bypass the local church, or just tell them what they must do in his name. Instead, he addresses them as the ones who must take responsibility'.[4]

Just as the task of removing members is exercised by the congregation, the church is also given the responsibility of welcoming people in. In Matthew 18, Jesus finishes his discussion on church discipline by saying, 'whatever you bind on earth will have been bound in heaven, and whatever you loose on earth will have been loosed in heaven' (v18). This language of binding and loosing has already been used in Matthew's gospel when Jesus says to Peter, 'I will give you the keys of the kingdom of heaven, and whatever you bind on earth will have been bound in heaven, and whatever you loose on earth will have been loosed in heaven' (16:19). This exercise of the keys of the kingdom is given to the church in Matthew 18. Whatever they bind and loose on earth will be bound or loosed in Heaven.

How, then, are these 'keys' to be exercised? We have already seen one way in Matthew 18. The person removed from church membership is put out of the visible covenant community by the church. In Matthew 28:18–30, we see how the church affirms genuine disciples and brings them into the covenant community. Jesus calls the church to go into all the world, make disciples and

---

4 Ibid., p.197

identify them as believers by baptising them in his name. Those who are baptised into Christ are recognised as genuine disciples by the people to whom Jesus has delegated the authority to exercise the keys of the kingdom, the church. It makes perfect sense that the ones given the responsibility to remove people from the church would also have the authority to welcome new believers in. It is clear these responsibilities hang together and Jesus gives them both to the church. That is, the congregation determine who belongs.

What is taught

Writing to the churches in Galatia, Paul says 'I am amazed that you are so quickly turning away from him who called you by the grace of Christ and are turning to a different gospel – not that there is another gospel, but there are some who are troubling you and want to distort the gospel of Christ' (Gal. 1:6–7). It is notable that Paul does not write to the local bishop asking him to rein in the churches. He doesn't even write to the elders of the churches. He writes 'to the churches of Galatia' (1:2). That he really does mean the church as a whole, and not just its leadership, is clear in what he writes throughout the letter. He consistently refers to the churches in the second-person plural and highlights how they have been taken in by false teaching (cf. 1:6; 3:1–3; 4:19–20, etc.). Despite acknowledging that they are being led astray, Paul affirms that it is up to them as churches to maintain the right teaching of the gospel. In fact, in defending the gospel in their own churches, he says the congregation have more authority than either an apostle or an angel:

> But even if we or an angel from heaven should preach to you a gospel contrary to what we have preached to you, a curse be on him! As we have said before, I now say again: If anyone is preaching to you a gospel contrary to what you received, a curse be on him! (Gal. 1:8–9)

Paul is not arguing that the Galatian churches have more understanding of the gospel than he does. He calls them foolish for being led astray by false teachers (cf. 3:1)! What Paul is saying is that they, as churches, are *responsible* for defending the gospel. God has given the church this responsibility and delegated the necessary authority to them. The churches have already received and believed the gospel. As such, they are competent to defend it (Gal. 3:3–5) and Paul insists it is their responsibility to do so.

This is not unique to the churches in Galatia. In his first letter to the Corinthians, Paul says 'I want to make clear for you, brothers and sisters, the gospel which I preached to you, which you received, on which you have taken your stand and by which you are being saved, if you hold to the message I preached to you' (1 Cor. 15:1–2). The Corinthian church have taken their stand on the gospel that was proclaimed to them by Paul and are now responsible for continuing to hold to it. Similarly, John encourages the churches to welcome those who are rightly preaching the gospel (3 Jn. 5–8) and reject those who are teaching a false gospel (2 Jn. 7–11). Again, the responsibility for determining what is taught in the church – for defending the gospel and encouraging those who proclaim it – is given to the churches. It is to the church that John says, 'do not believe every spirit, but test the spirits to see if they are from God, because many false prophets have gone out into the world' (1 Jn. 4:1).

This makes perfect sense. We saw earlier the logical necessity that those given the responsibility to remove people from membership are the same ones to welcome people into the church. By the same token, those called to make sure the church does not depart from the gospel must also be the ones with the responsibility to ensure the gospel is taught faithfully. Jesus gave this responsibility to all his disciples in the Great Commission when he commanded them to 'Go, therefore, and make disciples of all nations, baptising them in the name of the Father and of the Son and of the Holy Spirit, *teaching them to observe everything I have commanded you*' (Mt. 28:19–20a, *my emphasis*). It is the task of the church to defend the gospel and to make sure that Jesus' teaching is properly passed on to new disciples.

Who leads

We see exactly the same pattern established concerning the choice of leaders in the church. Scripture gives the church the job of removing errant leaders, along with the corresponding responsibility to appoint new elders. Since the church is responsible for recognising genuine believers and for upholding right teaching of the word, it isn't surprising they are also tasked with appointing leaders who will have teaching responsibilities. These things naturally hang together.

As we said in the introduction, issues of polity and church structures rarely seem that important until, all of a sudden, there is a problem. There are few problems quite as serious as an eldership that have rejected the gospel. The question is, what is to be done about it? If there are no bishops to approach and outside bodies have no authority to reach into the church, who handles the issue? If elders appoint elders without reference to the church, and all the elders have departed from orthodoxy, there is no recourse. Has Jesus left his people helpless? Absolutely not!

The Bible gives a mechanism for the removal of errant leaders. 1 Timothy 5:19–21 says:

> Don't accept an accusation against an elder unless it is supported by two or three witnesses. Publicly rebuke those who sin, so that the rest will be afraid. I solemnly charge you before God and Christ Jesus and the elect angels to observe these things without prejudice, doing nothing out of favouritism.

Whilst these verses guard against vexatious accusations – no single member can simply accuse an elder of sin and have them removed on a whim – if an accusation against a leader is substantiated by witnesses, they are to be publicly rebuked in front of the church. The elders, just like every other church member, are not above church discipline. The process of witnesses followed by public rebuke if there is no repentance applies to member and elder alike.

If that public rebuke is ignored, the elder – just like any errant member – must be removed from fellowship. It is inconceivable that Paul's warnings to avoid those who teach false doctrine (cf. Rom. 16:17; Tit. 3:10) apply to everybody except the elders in that church. Similarly, John says in 2 John 9–11:

> Anyone who does not remain in Christ's teaching but goes beyond it does not have God. The one who remains in that teaching, this one has both the Father and the Son. If anyone comes to you and does not bring this teaching, do not receive him into your home, and do not greet him; for the one who greets him shares in his evil works.

It is difficult to see how welcoming false teachers from outside your church into your home means you are sharing in his evil works but allowing a false teacher to continue as an elder inside your church is not.

We also have Paul's comments to Timothy about false teachers in 1 Timothy 6:3–5:

> If anyone teaches false doctrine and does not agree with the sound teaching of our Lord Jesus Christ and with the teaching that promotes godliness, he is conceited and understands nothing, but has an unhealthy interest in disputes and arguments over words. From these come envy, quarrelling, slander, evil suspicions, and constant disagreement among people whose minds are depraved and deprived of the truth, who imagine that godliness is a way to material gain.

Whatever else we may say about these verses from 1 Timothy 6, it is clear that if the person being described is an elder in the local church, they are disqualified according to the criteria Paul outlines in 1 Timothy 3. Indeed, they ought to be removed from the church and, as we have seen already, the authority to remove individuals from fellowship lies with the church. Taken altogether, if the church are to publicly rebuke elders in unrepentant sin, have been given the authority to defend the gospel and are encouraged to have nothing to do with those who would teach a false gospel, it follows that the authority to remove errant elders rests with the church themselves.

By the same logic we employed earlier, if the authority to remove elders has been given to the church, it makes sense that they are also the ones called to recognise new elders. We have already seen in earlier chapters that the pattern of appointing people in the church laid down in Acts 1 and 6 involved the whole congregation. Paul and Barnabas 'appointing elders' in Acts 14 is used as shorthand for this process. David Peterson comments on the appointment of elders in Acts 14:23, 'The verb *cheirotonēsantes (appointed)* means "stretch out the hand" and came to be used of voting, choosing, and so appointment to office.'[5] By contrast, when Jesus appointed the Apostles, Mark 3:16 uses the word *poieō (make)* and Luke 6:13 the word *eklegomai (choose)*. The early church apparently appointed elders by gathering the whole congregation and agreeing the matter together through a vote.

These three areas of congregational responsibility are such that we must conclude the highest delegated authority in the church,

5 Peterson, D., *The Pillar New Testament Commentary: The Acts of the Apostles*, APOLLOS, Nottingham, UK, 2009, p.415

under Christ, is the congregation. The church is to be ruled by its members. It is to the church that Jesus gives the keys of the kingdom. It is the church members who determine who belongs, what is taught and who is to lead. They have the authority and responsibility from Jesus to remove and appoint their own leaders, to recognise their own members and to ensure right teaching of the word. The church is, therefore, to be ruled by its members.

This naturally throws up questions about the role of elders. If members rule, how on earth do elders lead? What is the relationship between elders and members? What does Jesus authorise elders to do?

Chapter 6:

The Position of the Elders

If the membership rules the church, it is reasonable to ask what position elders actually hold. Titus was left behind in Crete to help the churches appoint elders (Tit. 1:5). In Acts 14 we see Paul and Barnabas doing exactly the same (v23). Timothy and Titus are both given lists of qualifications to consider before the church appoints anyone as an elder (cf. 1 Tim. 3:1–17; Tit. 1:5–9). We also have to contend with the biblical language that goes along with eldership. Elders are called *overseers* (cf. Acts 20:28, Tit. 1:7, 1 Tim. 3:2, etc.) and are expected to handle at least some of the affairs of the church. The language of oversight and shepherding the flock clearly implies a leadership function. But how can elders lead when they don't hold ultimate authority in the church?

It is worth pointing out that these sorts of questions exist in most organisations with any sort of structure that relies on derived power and delegated authority. Think of the delegated authority a policeman has over the general public. In a roundabout way, in our Western democracy, it is the general public that has ultimate power over the average policeman. That officer is put into post by more senior police officials, who themselves are appointed by a Chief Constable, who is in turn answerable to government ministers, who are ultimately elected to power by the general public. Nevertheless, we all recognise the right of the ordinary bobby on the beat to arrest a member of the public who has broken the law. The power that our democracy places in the hands of the general public does not negate the delegated authority of the policeman to enforce the law. This is all part of good public order.

In a similar way, elders have delegated authority – given to them by Jesus – that operates under the rule of the church. We will look at exactly what he delegates to elders in the next few chapters. At this point, let's just note that congregational rule in local churches no more undermines the position of its elders than the rule of Christ undermines the delegated authority of either the congregation or its leaders. Just as with our police constable, along with anybody else listed in that circular chain of command, it is evidently possible to have real authority over others without ultimate rule.

Again, we see this in British law. Regardless of one's belonging or allegiance to the British crown or constitution, the logic of how power is exercised and delegated through these channels is a good illustration of how different kinds of authority can relate to one another. Constitutionally, the sovereign ruler of the United Kingdom is the reigning monarch. The one who sits on the throne has ultimate rule. But if you ask the average person on the street who makes our laws, who governs our country, who has the power to effect change, it is clear to most people that such power rests with elected members of parliament. Because the monarch is the sovereign ruler, all Acts of Parliament must be ratified by the Crown. The authority government ministers have is delegated from the Crown, and they exercise their authority in the name of the sovereign monarch. However, it is the government that actually makes the laws of the land and is the body that leads our country. There is a distinction between the authority to lead and the right to rule.

The British government lead with delegated authority from the Crown and are appointed to their role by the voting public. The right to vote and the right to form a government derive from the authority of the Crown according to an uncodified constitution. This mirrors the authority that elders have to lead, and church members have to appoint their leaders, which derives from the ultimate authority of King Jesus according to the Scriptures.

It is important to recognise that eldership authority in the church does not derive from the congregation. It is true that the congregation appoints elders in the local church, but the delegated authority exercised by elders comes not from the recognition of the church itself, but from Jesus, as outlined in the Scriptures. So, just as the Crown delegates the right to elect governments to the people, and the right to form government belongs to those elected to parliament, so the authority to appoint and remove leaders given to the congregation, and the right for elders to lead, are delegated areas of responsibility and authority all authorised by King Jesus.

Many people think of independent congregational polity along the lines shown in the following diagram:

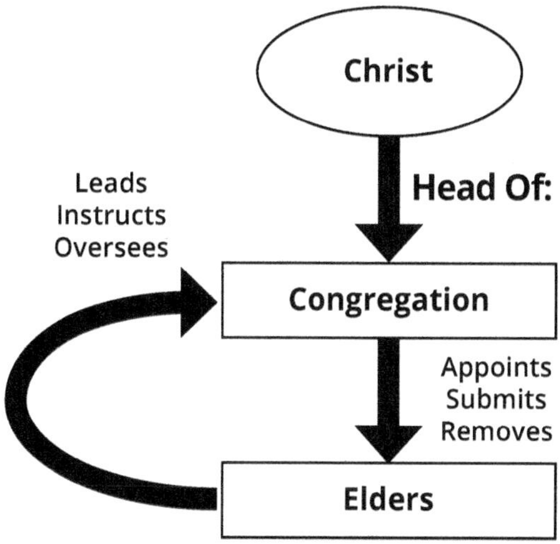

This helpfully shows that the church is under the lordship of Christ and explains that elders are appointed by the congregation. Unfortunately, the unhelpful message it conveys is that elders draw their authority from the congregation that appointed them. Biblically, this is not the case.

According to Scripture, the whole church is under the headship of Christ. Though the members rule, they rule under the authority of the Lord Jesus. The elders are genuinely appointed to lead, but they lead under the headship of Christ. Though the members rule, the elders nevertheless meaningfully lead. We can describe this as elder-led, member-ruled congregational polity. It is better pictured in the following diagram:

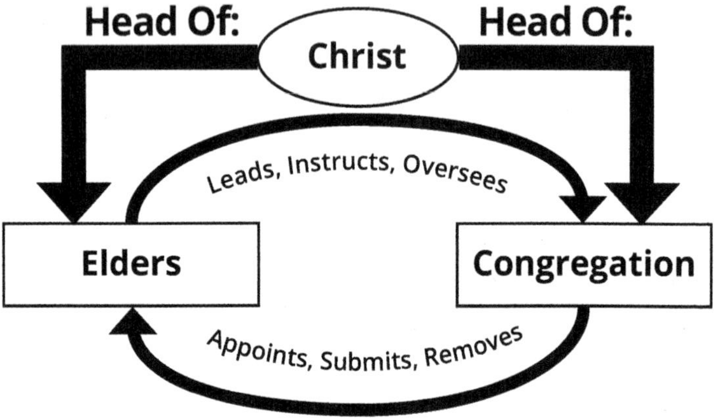

It is true that elders are appointed by the church to lead, but their responsibilities are given to them by Jesus. Their role derives from Scripture and comes from the delegated authority given to them by Christ. This is the same for the congregation. They are given their specific membership responsibilities by Jesus, and the authority they hold as the ruling body in the church is delegated to them by Christ, who is head over the whole church. The difference between the elders and the congregation is that Jesus delegates different roles and functions to them both.

Before we move on to think about what the specific responsibilities and functions are for elders, there are other structural matters to address. We have seen that elders are to lead under the rule of the members, but how many people should be appointed? Is one leader enough, or should there be more? Related to this, we have to ask whether there are specific offices to be filled or whether there are gifts to be recognised: is there a set number of people required to lead, or do we appoint as many elders as the Lord has chosen to give us?

Chapter 7:

Eldership as a Gift of Grace

How would you answer the following questions: is eldership an office in the church to be filled, with *elder* being the title that goes along with the position, or is eldership fundamentally a ministry function to be exercised by suitably gifted people? Should we think of elders as those who take office and lead the church, or should we think of them as men with particular gifts who are carrying out a ministry function in the service of the church? Maybe your answer is that you can't see much difference. But the reality is, how we answer these questions significantly impacts not only what we understand elders to be, but how they function, how many of them we need and how we go about appointing them.

The word *office* is never used in the New Testament to describe any function in the local church. Clifford Pond points out, 'It does appear in the Authorised Version in three places, but an examination of these texts will show that they import an idea that was not in Paul's mind.'[1] These three verses are Romans 11:13, 12:4 and 1 Timothy 3:1. We only have to look them up in any other translation to see that the word *office* is not used. As we noted in our chapter on independency, the King James Bible (that is, the Authorised Version) took some particular editorial decisions as a result of perceived challenges to the power of external church structures, especially the authority of the king, in versions such as the Tyndale Bible. The idea for the new translation came as a result of a conference in 1604 between the Puritans and King James. Michael Reeves says:

> James suspected that the Puritans were really angling for a Presbyterian church order… reform was all very well, but only so long as it did not involve chipping away at his divinely given authority as king. The Puritans came away with virtually nothing. The only significant Puritan idea that James did like was a new version of the Bible to be prepared. James' mind raced: at last he could be rid of those awkward marginal notes in the Geneva Bible that advocated such worrying things as disobedience to a bad king. And so King James' authorised version of the Bible was commissioned.[2]

This explains why the KJV prefers the word *office* despite context showing it is not the intended meaning of the word.

1 Pond, *Only Servants*, p.42

2 Reeves, M., *The Unquenchable Flame*, Inter-Varsity Press, London, UK, 2009, p.154

Only in 1 Timothy 3:1 do some other translations use the phrase *office of overseer* (see the ESV for example). However, the English wording *office of overseer* is a translation of the single Greek word *episkopē (overseer)*. This imports a view of offices that is not reflected in the text of the original language. The CSB more helpfully translates the verse in this way: 'This saying is trustworthy: "If anyone aspires to be an overseer, he desires a noble work."' This rightly avoids importing the word *office* where it does not exist. The New Testament knows nothing of people in the local church holding office.

Perhaps the biggest problem with viewing eldership as an office is that it leads us to believe there is a position that must be filled, much like electing an MP. At a General Election, parliament is prorogued and every member of the House of Commons loses their seat. The country then goes to the polls to elect new representatives because there are now 650 vacant spaces and someone must fill them. In a similar way, churches that view eldership as an office may well seek to appoint someone to fill the vacant space simply because churches need elders. But as we saw in our chapter on independency, legitimate local churches existed in the New Testament before there were any elders. Though it is not ideal, nor God's long-term plan, the church nevertheless can exist without elders. That is, a church remains a legitimate church even if no elders can be found. Returning to the example of the UK Parliament, it does not exist if there are no sitting MPs – these are offices that must be filled for government to both exist and function. Elders, however, are simply not imperative to the existence of biblical churches nor their legitimate functioning as churches in the same way.

Further, we have to recognise that the church is made up of members gifted by God to serve together in ministry. If we rightly understand the body imagery in Scripture, each member has a specific function. Nobody looks at a body, sees that it has no eyes, and decides it would be a good idea to graft a foot onto the face in the hope it will do the job. A foot simply cannot see for you. In the same way, it is a mistake to think that a church with unqualified elders in post will function better than a church without any elders at all. Just as a body without a finger will function far better than attempting to remove a knee from its place and then graft it on as a finger, so a church without elders – although incomplete and deformed – is better than unqualified men being shoehorned into a role they are incapable of filling.

If we recognise that eldership is not an office but a ministry function of those gifted by God to do it, we have to see the sovereignty of God at work in this. Just as nobody can appoint a Head of the Church – but must recognise Christ as the only one who can undertake that ministry – so it is not the church's job to create elders, but to recognise those gifted by God for the task. In the list of biblical qualifications for eldership in Titus 1 and 1 Timothy 3, it is notable that there is only one discernible skill or ability among them. What we are looking for when it comes to elders is not so much people with great talents but men of particular character. Such character is a matter of spiritual growth effected by the Holy Spirit, and not primarily a question of special abilities. That is to say,

God gifts his church with suitable elders and the church recognises such men.

It is also worth remembering the doctrine of the priesthood of all believers that we briefly sketched out earlier. All believers are gifted by God to minister in some way within the church. The whole church should be involved in the work of ministry. The priesthood of all believers stops us from assuming the elders, or worse a single pastor, should be doing all the work whilst the 'laity' feeds off the 'clergy'. Every member of the church is a minister of the gospel and should be involved in its work, as part of an interconnected body, each of whom – elder and member alike – feeds on Christ. Just as the church recognises people who are gifted for other areas of ministry, so the church should recognise those who have been suitably gifted by God for the ministry of eldership. If the whole body is serving and using their gifts for the benefit of the church to the glory of God, we should be able to recognise those who have been gifted by God to lead, as we see them serve, minister and effectively do the work of eldership, even before they have been formally recognised and set apart for it by the church.

In 1 Corinthians 12, Paul tells the church that all their members are gifted for ministry. He says, 'you are the body of Christ, and individual members of it. And God has appointed these in the church: first apostles, second prophets, third teachers, next miracles, then gifts of healing, helping, leading, various kinds of tongues' (v27–28). Notice here, Paul says that it is God who has appointed these ministers in the church, even those who are 'helping'. Earlier in the same chapter, Paul says, 'There are different ministries, but the same Lord. And there are different activities, but the same God works all of them in each person' (vv5–6). These are gifts that God has distributed among the church. The whole church is to minister to one another in the functions God has given them. Indeed, the entire metaphor is not about abilities and talents but roles, functions and ministries for the church.[3] It's worth noting here: Apostles, prophets and teachers are all considered ministries and functions gifted by God to the church, just like all the other gifts that follow.

Similarly, in Ephesians 4:11, Paul says that Jesus 'gave some to be apostles, some prophets, some evangelists, some pastors and teachers.' We will see later the link between the terms *pastor*, *elder* and *overseer*, but at this point, let's just notice that it is Christ himself who appoints pastors and teachers to the church. Given the connection drawn in 1 Timothy 5:17 between elders and those who labour in preaching and teaching, it is not a stretch to read eldership into Ephesians 4:11 where it mentions pastor-teachers. The point is that it is Jesus himself who gives elders to the church. He distributes gifts to the members and fits people for service in appropriate ministries. It is biblically justified, then, to understand eldership less as an office to be filled and more as a spiritual ministry that Jesus gifts to the church by fitting particular people to fulfil that function.

This fitting for ministry and appointment to service is not unique to elders. The four word-ministry functions in Ephesians

---

3 For more on the biblical use of the word gift and gifting along with an extended discussion on why we should understand the lists of spiritual gifts as ministries and functions for the church see Berding, K., *What Are Spiritual Gifts? Rethinking The Conventional View*, Kregel Publications, Wheaton, Illinois, 2006, p.75–6

4:11 were all appointments recognised by the community. That is why prophets and apostles were attested by signs and marks of authenticity (cf. Deut. 13:1–5, 18:22; 2 Cor. 12:12). The local church has been given the authority to determine what is taught and who can teach, so evangelists, pastors and teachers are affirmed by the community of saints; they are recognised as qualified by the church. Even in the list of ministry functions in 1 Corinthians 12, an individual is usually recognised as fit for that ministry and appointed to serve by the elders who have been recognised to oversee the church and its ministry. The point being, Jesus distributes gifts to his church and it is for the church to recognise the gifts he has given and appoint people to fulfil appropriate ministry functions that make best use of them.

Nevertheless, it's clear that the church is supposed to appoint its own elders. The question is, how many elders does the church need?

Chapter 8:

Putting a Number on Gifts of Grace

If the church is to formally recognise those who have been gifted for eldership by God, we are still left with the question of just how many elders we need. Based on what we have seen so far, the answer is that we don't need any at all if by *need* we mean to exist as a legitimate church. We have already seen that New Testament churches existed legitimately *before* any elders were appointed. So, to be a legitimate local church, elders of themselves are not essential. We've also seen, just as it is better to have no foot than to stitch on inappropriate body parts that cannot do the job, it is better to have no elders than to appoint unqualified men to fulfil a function they cannot perform. If this is what we mean when we ask how many elders we *need*, the answer is ultimately *none*.

Of course, we also saw that this was not God's ultimate design for the church: it isn't ideal and neither is it good. The Bible clearly calls us to appoint elders. So, perhaps a better question is not how many elders do we *need*, but how many elders does God want us to have? I carefully word the question that way because what people often want to know is, how many elders must a church appoint? For the answer to that, I refer you back to the opening paragraph of this chapter. But how many elders does God want us to have? That is a slightly different question to which there are two biblical answers. The first and simplest of which is: more than one.

It is impossible to avoid the clear pattern of plural eldership in Scripture. The very first mention of elders in the local church comes in Acts 11:30. The church in Antioch wanted to send famine relief and to give it to the elders (plural) in the Jerusalem church to distribute. Likewise, when Paul and Barnabas go to Jerusalem concerning the false gospel that has come out of Judea in Acts 15, there are five instances of the phrase 'apostles and elders' (plural) (cf. vv2,4,6,22,23). This continues in 16:4 when the decision of the 'apostles and elders at Jerusalem' is relayed to other churches. Every mention of elders in Jerusalem comes in the plural. It is impossible to avoid the fact that there was definitely more than one elder in the Jerusalem church.

We have already looked at Acts 14:23: Paul and Barnabas 'appointed elders ... in every church.' Though we considered this fact earlier in relation to the process of appointing elders, here it is worth noting that each local church had elders (plural) appointed in them. Similarly, Paul instructed Titus to appoint elders (plural) in the churches in Crete (Titus 1:5). The pattern set and the instruction given is to appoint multiple elders in individual churches.

In his farewell address to the Ephesians in Acts 20:17 'Paul sent for the elders of the church'. Again, we see multiple elders.[1] Similarly, in Acts 21 when Paul goes to see James in Jerusalem, we are told 'all the elders were present' (v18). Every mention of local church elders in Acts comes in the plural and shows multiple elders within each individual congregation.

Further, Paul says to Timothy, 'The elders who are good leaders are to be considered worthy of double honour, especially those who work hard at preaching and teaching' (1 Tim. 5:17). This comment fits with the evidence in Acts that local churches had plural eldership. Similarly, when Paul writes to the Philippians he greets the 'overseers and deacons' (plural; 1:1). Although the word *elders* isn't used here, given the non-existence of external oversight over local churches the term *overseer* refers to those with oversight *within* the local church and is synonymous with the word *elder*. Finally, we see James instruct those who are sick to 'call for the elders [plural] of the church [singular]' (5:14) and Peter writes a particular section of his first letter to 'the elders [plural] among you' (5:1).

Almost every example we have in the New Testament concerning local church elders comes in the plural. There are only three examples of *elder* being used in the singular, but these refer either to one elder writing a particular letter (cf. 2 Jn. 1; 3 Jn. 1)

---

1 Some posit that this represents a group of elders overseeing multiple churches in Ephesus. However, when there are multiple churches in a region, Paul writes 'to the churches in ...' whereas it seems, when there is only one church in an area, he writes 'to the church in ...' or similar. Given the pattern we have of multiple elders in each local church, it seems best to view it as one local church in Ephesus with multiple elders in it.

or concerns an accusation against a specific elder (1 Tim. 5:19). These instances do not undercut or contradict the univocal voice of Scripture. As Jeramie Rinne says, 'Again and again we find elders (plural) in each church (singular).'[2] Based on this pattern, the first and simplest answer to how many elders God wants us to have is: more than one.

However, though the pattern of Scripture is multiple elders in single churches, there is nothing expressly commanded concerning the number of elders to appoint. This makes some sense because clearly the planting of new churches, which are biblically legitimate, will take some time before elders can be appointed. Moreover, as we saw earlier, eldership is not fundamentally an office to be filled but a ministry to be undertaken by men who are suitably gifted by God. It is for the church to recognise qualified elders, but it is ultimately the Lord himself who gifts elders to the church. This is why we carefully worded our question at the start of this chapter.

Given that local churches legitimately existed *without* elders, and the church is called to recognise the men gifted to them by God, we have to surmise that the pattern of multiple elders in local churches is the biblical model God intends for us to follow and towards which we ought to be working. That does not mean we should appoint unqualified elders to ensure we are biblically compliant. Appointing unqualified elders would be to disobey what is expressly commanded in 1 Timothy 3:1–7 and Titus 1:5–9. Just as it is unbiblical to appoint an unsuitable man as an elder because there is no elder yet in place, so it is also unbiblical to appoint an

---

2 Rinne, J, *Church Elders: How To Shepherd God's People Like Jesus*, Crossway, Weaton, Illinois, 2014, p.88

unsuitable man as an elder to ensure plurality. Furthermore, it would mean ignoring God's sovereign provision in order to do something that is not actually commanded explicitly, but rather established as a model to which the church must aspire. All of that is to say, the second and slightly more nuanced answer to our question about how many elders God wants us to appoint is: it depends.

In God's sovereignty, a church may have no suitable elders. Think of a church where a handful of elderly folks, mainly older ladies, rely on visiting speakers each week because none of their members are suitably qualified elders.[3] Much could be said about this scenario but the bottom line is, they have no business appointing somebody the Lord has expressly told them not to appoint because they do not meet the qualifications for eldership laid out in his word. If he has not gifted them with anybody suitable, then, such as they are a legitimate church, they must be so without elders. They ought to aspire to a plurality. Biblically, they should be working towards that end. But for the time being, they have no elders to appoint, so they must accept that this is the Lord's provision for them at this time. There may be some questions they want to ask themselves: why they are in this position, is it tenable to carry on under the circumstances and how likely is it that these things will develop into a biblically healthy position in future? However they answer such questions, they cannot formally recognise people that God has not yet gifted to the church.

Other churches may be labouring on with a lone pastor. My predecessor at Oldham Bethel Church was in exactly this position. He would have been biblically in the wrong if he was entirely happy

---

3 I have known of churches in exactly this position.

with that setup and had no desire to do anything about it. He would have been all the more wrong, however, if he had, in a desperate bid to create plural eldership, appointed people who were unqualified for the role. The result would have been more disastrous than simply acknowledging that plurality was impossible at that point in time. The fact is, the Lord – in his sovereignty – gifted the church with one suitable elder. There were efforts underway to address that, and, in the Lord's providence, he gave the church suitable people so they could appoint more than one elder in time.

The biblical model of plural eldership in every church is not explicitly commanded in Scripture but is a matter to which the church must aspire. By contrast, the qualifications for eldership are explicitly commanded. The counter to this is the instruction to Titus to 'appoint elders', but it seems likely – as we have seen previously – that it came with the implicit proviso that such men must be suitably qualified and available. That is, after all, why Paul gave Titus eldership qualifications to adhere to in the first place. The church should be looking for multiple elders and working towards plurality, without discarding the biblical qualifications. They need to recognise that it is the Lord himself who will gift such people to the church as he sees fit.

At the other end of the spectrum, what about a much larger church? I was once invited to spend a week at a church with 1000 members or so (not in the UK), which had over 50 elders. The question is, is that too many? When the pastor of that church was at a UK conference he was asked this question: how many elders is appropriate? His answer: appoint as many elders as God has gifted to your church. Why would God give you such gifts among your people and not expect you to use them? He was further asked, what if you don't have suitably qualified people to appoint? His answer: take it up with the Holy Spirit! If he hasn't seen fit to give you those gifts, that is his prerogative. This is a good and biblically consistent answer.

In his book, 40 *Questions About Elders and Deacons*, Benjamin Merkle lays out three common ways churches frequently address this question. Based on what we have seen above, his description of the 'open system' seems to be the most biblically faithful. He states:

> Some churches opt for a more open approach and do not specify the number of elders they should have or a certain ratio. If there is a perceived need for more elders, the church will pray that God will provide them with gifted and suitably qualified men. An advantage to this approach is that it focuses more on letting God provide the right people rather than seeking to fill an empty position.[4]

What we are aiming for is a plurality of elders, but we recognise we can only appoint whomever God has gifted to us. We cannot put a ratio on God's grace or demand that he gives us what he, in his sovereignty, has determined not to grant. In the end, it is better to have no elders than unfit ones. But as a matter of principle, it is God's design for individual local churches to have multiple elders and this is what we at least ought to be working towards.

---

4 Merkle, 40 *Questions*, p.168

If the pattern for local church eldership is plural, what is the relationship between the elders? Are we justified in viewing the pastor as a higher spiritual authority than the other elders? Can the pastor outvote other elders? Should we consider the pastor to be 'first amongst equals'? These are the questions we will think about next.

Chapter 9:

Plural Eldership and Parity

If the biblical model of church leadership is multiple elders in individual churches, how are those elders supposed to relate to one another? Is it legitimate to have one elder – probably the pastor – who is 'first amongst equals'? Is it biblical for one elder to have a greater voice than the others? Are there different types of elder, with one kind more senior than another?

Some insist that 1 Timothy 5:17 creates two kinds of office. Louis Berkhof, for example, argues that 'elders were not originally teachers' with later circumstances leading to 'a distinction between the elders or overseers that were entrusted only with the government of the Church, and those who were called upon to teach'.[1] As such, Presbyterian Churches believe in two eldership roles: 'one may be set apart as a "teaching elder" to minister the word and sacraments in distinction from the other "ruling" elders who share effective

1 Berkhof, *Systematic Theology*, p.586

leadership with him'.[2] This position isn't unique to Presbyterians. Peter Masters – long-time pastor at the Metropolitan Tabernacle in London – insists there are different offices within the eldership: '(1) the minister or pastor as the preaching elder. (In larger churches there could be more than one.) (2) the ruling elders. These are assisting, shepherding elders exercising a ministry of teaching and counselling other than the public ministry of the word, and sharing the work of discipline and care with their pastor, who is the presiding elder.'[3] The Apostle Paul talks about the honour due to elders 'who are good leaders' and then adds 'especially those who work hard at preaching and teaching' (1 Tim. 5:17). There is clearly a distinction drawn here but, as Benjamin Merkle says, 'This small chasm... has become a great gulf according to the distinctions that are made by some.'[4]

The primary problem with this view of 1 Timothy 5:17 is the qualifications for eldership themselves in 1 Timothy 3 and Titus 1. If the distinction Paul makes is between 'teaching elders' and 'ruling elders', why does he insist in 1 Timothy 3 that *all* the elders must be 'able to teach' (3:2)? Indeed, Titus 1:9 says an elder must hold 'to the faithful message as taught, so that he will be able both to encourage with sound teaching and to refute those who contradict it.' If there is such a thing as ruling elders distinct from teaching elders, why does 1 Timothy 3:2 insist they must be able to teach when they aren't expected to teach anybody? Why does Titus 1:9 suggest they must be able to 'encourage with sound teaching' when they aren't

2 Milne, *Know The Truth*, p.242

3 As quoted in Pond, *Only Servants*, p.51

4 Merkle, *40 Questions*, p.85

expected to do any teaching? In light of these qualifications, it seems profoundly unlikely that Paul is distinguishing two types of elder based on their ability to teach.

It seems more likely that Paul is simply acknowledging the reality that some elders will do more of the teaching than others. The distinction cannot be between those who are able to teach and those who cannot because all elders must have that ability in order to be qualified for the role. Rather, Paul seems to be making a distinction based on time devoted to teaching. Matthew Henry says of 1 Timothy 5:17: 'they had not, in the primitive church, one to preach to them and another to rule them, but ruling and teaching were performed by the same persons. The work of ministers consists principally in two things: ruling well and labouring in the word and doctrine.'[5] 1 Timothy 5:17 tells us that some elders will spend more time labouring in preaching and teaching than others. As Samuel Waldron says, 'The contrast is not between no teaching and teaching. It is between some teaching and a greater degree of teaching.'[6] Paul does not give us the specific reasons why one elder may teach more than another – any such suggestions are mere conjecture – but he does suggest some elders may do more teaching than others.

Other arguments advanced for distinct preaching and teaching elders concern the authority of the word in the life of the church. Clifford Pond summarises this argument: 'If this authority is to be

---

5 Church, L.F. (ed), *Matthew Henry's Commentary on the Whole Bible*, Marshall, Morgan and Scott, London, 1960, p.689

6 Waldron, S., 'Plural-Elder Congregationalism' in *Who Runs The Church? 4 Views on Church Government*, ed. Engle, P.E. & Cowan, S.B., Zondervan, Grand Rapids, 2004, p.81

exercised, then those who teach and preach the word must have a special role above the other elders, normally called ruling elders.'[7] Whilst it is certainly true that the word is central to the authority given to elders, any distinction melts away when we see – as we have argued above – *all* elders are required to be able to teach. All elders, therefore, have a hand in the teaching of the local church. If being able to teach is fundamental to the work of eldership, then the centrality of the word has no impact on the authority of any given elder because all are apt to teach. Even if one elder takes on more of the teaching than the others, their teaching does not carry greater authority in the life of the church than that of other elders. Nor does their opinion or interpretation of Scripture carry more weight than that of other elders, who are also able to teach and rightly handle the word of God. Their authority does not derive from the *amount* of teaching they do, but from their qualification and ability to rightly handle the word.

Some want to argue for a 'senior pastor' position that carries greater weight amongst the eldership. Such a pastor, they argue, may well be better qualified, works full-time for the church and is devoted to the ministry of the word. However, this effectively creates a two-tier eldership not entirely unlike the teaching and ruling distinction favoured by Presbyterianism. As Jeramie Rinne points out, this is not just an issue concerning 'Senior' pastors, but 'somehow, somewhere along the way, we have differentiated pastors from elders, the paid ministry pros from the unpaid trustees. But the New Testament makes no such distinction.'[8] The Bible does not

7 Pond, *Only Servants*, p.52

8 Rinne, *Church Elders*, p.32

seem to recognise this two-fold approach to the office of elder but instead calls for parity between elders, including the pastor.

Scripture uses the terms *elder*, *pastor* and *overseer* interchangeably to describe the same role and function within the church (cf. Acts 20:17,28; Tit. 1:5,7; 1 Pet. 5:1-2). When Paul sent for the elders at Ephesus, he sent for all of them together, not just for a single senior leader (Acts 20:17). He goes on to exhort all the elders in Ephesus to care for the church and watch over the flock (Acts 20:28). When Timothy was commissioned by the church, it was the council of elders who sent him off together (1 Tim. 4:14). When James tells the sick to call for the elders, he either expects any one of the elders to be able to carry out the task equally or he thinks all the elders must carry out this function together. But it is clear he doesn't expect only the pastor to be able to pray for the sick (Jas. 5:14). Peter's exhortations are to all the elders of the local church, not just a senior pastor. He is clear that all the elders are to equally exercise oversight, shepherd the flock and to have younger members subject to them (1 Pet. 5:1–5). All these things point to equality of responsibility, authority and status within an eldership.

This means that all elders are to have parity of esteem, and no one elder should sit above the others. The fact of the matter is that all elders must meet the same qualifications. There are no eldership qualifications that are distinct from those of a pastor. Similarly, the responsibilities given to all elders – specifically teaching and ruling – are the same responsibilities of a pastor. If all elders must meet the same criteria and fulfil the same responsibilities, there is no reason to distinguish between senior and subordinate forms of eldership or between pastors and elders. There is similarly no biblical basis for distinguishing between the authority of elders based on their being full-time or part-time, paid or unpaid. Though 1 Timothy 5:17 establishes the legitimate principle of financially supporting elders for the purposes of ministry, it does not give a greater degree of authority to those who are remunerated. If the pastor holds more authority in the church than the elders, then an unbiblical distinction has been made between them. Alexander Strauch is surely right when he says, '[this] will, at least in practice, *create a separate, superior office over the eldership, just as was done in the early second century when the division between "the overseer" and "elders" occurred.*'[9] Every elder in the local church is equal in value, status, power and authority, and no distinction should be made between them in this regard.

Given his agreement on the status of elders, and his insistence that there should be no distinction between the pastor and the elders, it is surprising to find that Strauch nevertheless argues for a 'first amongst equals' model. It is difficult to see how such an approach doesn't just as easily 'create a separate, superior office over the eldership' in practice. Moreover, the biblical case for 'first amongst equals' rests on shaky ground to say the least. There is a claim that Peter, James and John were singled out for special attention by Jesus and, amongst the three, Peter in particular. Benjamin Merkle argues, 'Peter was often singled out and given special leadership. Because of his gifts and calling, he was the most

9 Strauch, A., *Biblical Eldership: An Urgent Call to Restore Biblical Church Leadership*, Lewis and Roth, Littleton, Colorado, 1995, pp.47-48, italics original

prominent among the apostles.'[10] Augustine of Hippo cites the keys of the kingdom as one such example.

However, the concept of 'first amongst equals' arose from Catholic doctrine that wants to argue Peter was the first Bishop of Rome, that is – the first Pope. This is based on his confession of Jesus as the Christ and the Lord's subsequent statement that 'you are Peter, and on this rock I will build my church' (Mt. 16:18). This is the point at which Peter is given the keys of the kingdom. But Jesus' statement was fulfilled in Acts 2 when Peter first preached the gospel in Jerusalem, not in any office he was granted. Further, though Jesus gives the keys of the kingdom to Peter first, as we have already seen, he later insists they belong to the rest of the Apostles too and then to the entire church. Given this, it is hard to see how it creates an exceptional leadership role when the entire church membership is given the same authority.

There are particular examples of Peter's leadership being overruled. At the meeting between the Jerusalem and Antioch Church in Acts 15, though Peter is clearly involved and significant in events, there is no escaping the fact that it is James – an elder in the church – who has the final word. James' leadership is primary in Acts 15, not Peter's. We also see Paul later confront Peter over his behaviour that was undercutting the gospel (cf. Gal. 2:11–21). Again, Peter's leadership was not in any way decisive here but rather it was Paul's leadership that, if such can be said at all, was primary. Though some make much of Peter being named first in the lists of Apostles in the gospels, it is notable that when Paul mentions the 'pillars of the church' in Galatians 2, it is James the brother of Jesus who

10 Merkle, 40 *Questions*, p.174

is named first, ahead of both Peter and John. Whether we should make that much of the order of these lists is questionable, but if we are going to, we must contend with James being mentioned ahead of Peter by Paul. Despite arguing Peter was 'first amongst equals', Benjamin Merkle notes: 'Yet, Peter was an Apostle just like the rest of the twelve. *He was never given a special title*. He did not wear different clothes or receive a higher salary. The others were not subordinate to him or function as his attendants or servants. He was equal in rank and authority to the rest of the Apostles' (my emphasis added).[11] To which I say, yes! Given all that, I see no ground to credibly argue Peter – or any elder after him – could be considered a 'first among equals'.

Even if we concede that Peter was 'first amongst equals' among the Apostles – and for the reasons outlined I see no reason to concede this point – why assume that what applied amongst the Apostles should be applied to elders at any rate? In the same way as we do not insist there must be twelve elders of every church because there were twelve Apostles, even if Jesus did apply a 'first amongst equals' approach to Peter, there is no evidence this is appropriate for pastors within an eldership. As already discussed, it is a category error to assume that what held for Apostles must necessarily hold within an eldership. It is difficult enough to justify a 'first amongst equals' model scripturally even when it comes to the Apostles themselves but when weighed against the biblical case for parity among elders, there is even less reason to argue that 'first amongst equals' must apply to an eldership. If we think terms such as 'Senior Pastor' create an artificial distinction between elders that

11 Ibid., p.174

represents an unbiblical hierarchy, how much more will imbuing the pastor with the authority of 'first amongst equals' lead to the same? Indeed, the only time an elder is ever described as *first* in Scripture is Diotrephes in 3 John, and it is certainly not a positive reference! If we are convinced that there should be parity amongst elders, there can be no first, there are only equals.

Chapter 10:

The Functions and Responsibilities of Elders

Essentially, elders have one job. There are various ways the Bible tells them to carry it out, but fundamentally, there is one task. The ultimate responsibility of all elders is to care for the spiritual needs of the church members.

As an elder, the scariest verse in the whole of Scripture is Hebrews 13:17. I am not saying this for rhetorical effect. It is, hand on heart, a verse that keeps me up at night and makes me break out in cold sweats. Members, of course, tend to focus on the instruction to 'obey your leaders and submit to them'. That, frankly, is the easy bit. The scary part is, 'since they [your elders] keep watch over your souls *as those who will give an account*' (my emphasis). What do elders have to account to the Lord for? How they have cared for the souls of church members! The Lord will ask every elder what they have done to serve the eternal good of those under their care. Did their instructions and example lead people to Jesus and help them become more like him or did they push people away from Christ and hinder their Christian walk? It is given to elders – who Jesus will call to account – to oversee the discipleship, growth and spiritual good of their church members. This is the one essential function of an elder. But when we look at this through the lens of Hebrews 13:17, that one task seems more than enough!

Paul puts it this way to the Ephesian elders: 'Be on guard for yourselves and for all the flock of which the Holy Spirit has appointed you as overseers, to shepherd the church of God, which he purchased with his own blood' (Acts 20:28). As in other parts of the New Testament (cf. 1 Pet. 5:1–4), three terms are brought together in the same verse here. Paul is speaking to the Ephesian elders, so we know these things apply to each of them. He says these *elders* have been appointed as *overseers*, so there is no distinction to be drawn between elders and overseers. The elders do the work of overseeing the members. He also refers to church members as a *flock* (Gk. *poimnion*) which the elders are to *shepherd* (Gk. *poimainō*). It is not hard to see how Paul is applying the language of being a *pastor* (Gk. *poimēn*, shepherd) to all the church elders. This verse shows us the terms elder, pastor and overseer are all synonymous and refer to the same function within the church. But it also describes eldership as a ministry of oversight, guarding the church membership from spiritual harm.

There are three key ways in which elders are to shepherd the flock. The Bible speaks about teaching the word, leading by example and equipping the members. Let's look at each in turn.

1) Teaching the word

There is only one skill, ability or talent listed in the qualifications for eldership. 1 Timothy 3:2 says (seventh in a list of criteria): an elder must be 'able to teach'. Titus 1:9 expands on this (the last qualification in that list): an elder must hold to 'the faithful message as taught, so that he will be able both to encourage with sound teaching and to refute those who contradict it.' Paul insists elders must be able to teach the word and do so in such a way that they can adequately encourage believers with it and competently refute those who depart from it. As Jeramie Rinne puts it, 'if elders shepherd Jesus's sheep, then their most basic task is to feed the souls of church members from the Scriptures. Without food, sheep weaken and die, and without regular nourishment through biblical teaching, Christians starve spiritually.'[1]

In Ephesians 4:11, Paul speaks about different ministries of the church: 'he himself gave some to be apostles, some prophets, some evangelists, some pastors and teachers.' There are three connected points worth noticing. First, these are all word-ministries. Apostles were given the job of passing on Jesus' teaching, prophets delivered God's words, evangelists proclaim the good news of the gospel and pastors teach local churches. Second, each of these roles is gifted to the church by Jesus. So, all the word-ministries of the church – note especially the role of pastors – are gifted to the church by Jesus. Third, the terms pastors and teachers go together in the Greek. In fact, many have commented the term is more properly understood as *pastor-teacher* – one function. Taken altogether, we

1 Rinne, *Church Elders*, p.45

can conclude that being a local church elder (remember, pastor and elder are synonymous terms) is a word-based ministry. Elders shepherd the flock through the teaching of the word.

There are three basic functions of this word ministry. First, it is to build up the church. In Ephesians 4:12–16, Paul tells us that elders shepherd the church by teaching the word and instructing the members in sound doctrine in order to build them up in the faith and bring them to maturity in Christ. Second, an elder's word ministry is to equip the saints for works of service. This is specifically what Ephesians 4:12 lands on: elders are to teach the word so that the members can effectively serve. You will be best equipped to share the gospel when you understand key Christian doctrine. You will be able to serve the members most helpfully when you understand Scripture and can apply it meaningfully in discipleship. Elders equip the church through the word. Third, elders shepherd the church through the word by calling back strays. When members are beginning to go astray, we shepherd the ones who are heading in the wrong direction with the word. We call people back to Christ through the word. We employ church discipline and equip the church to do it well, by the word.

If you are an elder, you are necessarily called to be a teacher, but that does not mean only fine preachers may be appointed. All elders must be able to teach; that much is clear from 1 Timothy 3:2. But the reason for that ability is given in Titus 1:9: elders must be able to encourage with sound teaching and refute those who deny it. Now, of course, it is possible to encourage with sound teaching from the pulpit, but that is clearly not the only place where that can and should happen. Likewise refuting those who deny sound teaching: whilst you can do it a bit from the pulpit, that is clearly not the only – nor even the primary – place this will happen. In Acts 15, when Paul and Barnabas were faced with men from Judea peddling a false gospel, they 'engaged them in serious argument and debate' (15:2). It seems quite unlikely that this was happening midway through a sermon. The point is that elders must know the gospel and have a solid understanding of Christian doctrine so that they are able to clearly communicate it to others. But there is nothing in this qualification that demands an excellent preacher. There is more than one way to teach sound doctrine and more than one forum in which to encourage believers and refute heretics. We shouldn't read 'able to teach' as 'great at preaching' – these are not the same thing.

It has become increasingly common for pastors to be viewed as *de facto* counsellors today. It is not at all uncommon to hear people insist that somebody is an excellent Bible teacher but not very 'pastoral'. Biblically, this does not compute. Pastors shepherd through the word. They lead by teaching the word. They may do that from the front in the pulpit, in Bible studies elsewhere or by informally applying the Scriptures to people's lives. Whatever the forum, the task of pastoring God's people is to teach the word and apply it to the situations of the people in front of us. The very act of sitting with someone, reading the Scriptures and showing them '*this* is what *that* is saying you ought to do in your particular situation' is the very definition of being pastoral. Yet, what people often want – and mean when they say *pastoral* – is that they want a personal counsellor.

Helpful as counselling can be, that is not the fundamental task of pastoral ministry nor a qualification for being a church elder. We are not called to minister as those able to soothe troubled minds nor are we called to be a sounding board for people's problems. For this, you need a psychiatrist or qualified counsellor, not a pastor. As someone who has written a book about mental health[2], and who still suffers from depressive illness and is a serving pastor, I know most elders and pastors are not qualified to deal with these things. Elders are qualified as those able to teach sound doctrine and apply the Scriptures to people's lives. That is the biblical requirement on them; it is what they are appointed to do, and it is how elders shepherd the church of God. Elders are, fundamentally, teachers.

The problem is that many confuse pastoring with counselling. Counsellors exist to help people frame and manage their internal, subjective perspectives on the world. They help people to explore their thoughts, feelings and behaviours as a means of addressing emotional and psychological issues. Counsellors do not give you their own opinions and advice; they help you find your own solutions to your problems. They are reflective listeners aiming to help you think through your issues and resolve them yourself. By contrast, elders are shepherds who shepherd by teaching the word and instructing God's people in what he says. They give us God's perspective on ourselves, how we should relate to him and how we should relate to the world. They bring the objective, external word of God to bear on our lives. They point to what God says and

2 Kneale, S. (ed.), *The pastor with a thorn in his side: stories of ministering with depression and what the church can do to help*, Grace Publications, 2021

apply the Scriptures to our lives in ways that are binding because, if they're right, God has said these things and wants you to respond rightly to them. Counsellors reflect; pastors instruct. If someone tells you what you should do, they are not offering counselling. If someone fails to tell you what God's word says you should think, feel or do, they are not pastoring.

This is why it is so important to understand what elders are qualified to do and what counsellors are qualified to do. To put it bluntly, pastors simply aren't trained to do what counsellors are trained to do and most of them are not capable of doing it. If you need someone to listen to you and help you rationalise your thoughts and emotions, a trained counsellor is what you need. Counsellors will serve you best when you need an outside party to help you rationalise your perspective and realise solutions to your emotional and psychological problems. By contrast, pastors will serve you best when you want to know what God's word says, how it applies to you and what you need to do in relation to it. They will point you to Jesus through his word and instruct you in what he says. There is nothing more pastoral than a pastor telling you exactly what God's word says to you, about you and for you.

I realise this is a huge topic. Space doesn't allow us to do it justice here and nor is it within this book's remit. By only touching upon it, I don't wish to oversimplify or dismiss the issues involved; quite the opposite! I hope to flag it up as a serious and significant issue which should not be glossed over. Instead, it should be given the time and space it deserves in a book of its own.

2) Leading by example

If the only skill or ability qualification for elders is 'able to teach', it bears asking what about the rest of the biblical qualifications listed in 1 Timothy 3 and Titus 1? All of them can be categorised as exemplars. They are things like being hospitable, not getting drunk, not being greedy, etc. None of them are what you would describe as skills or talents. They are all character traits and the stuff of everyday life that model what it is to be a godly Christian.

What is perhaps most interesting is that all these eldership qualifications are in fact expected of *every* believer, not just of church elders. Don Carson puts it this way:

> These verses teach us that the primary characteristic of the Christian elder/pastor/overseer is that his life constantly reflects Christian values, morality, conduct, and integrity ... there is nothing about superior IQ, charisma, powerful personality or the like. The Christian minister is supposed to be gentle, not supposed to get drunk, and so forth: the list is remarkable for being unremarkable. Indeed, with only a couple of exceptions, all of the qualifications listed here are elsewhere in the New Testament demanded of all Christians. For instance, this elder is supposed to be given to hospitality. But that is demanded of all Christians in Hebrews 13. What this means, then, is that the Christian pastor must exemplify

> in his own life the virtues and graces that are demanded of all the people of God.[3]

All the qualifications for eldership are demanded of all believers. Even in the case of not being a new convert, no one in the church should remain a novice forever; all are called to grow up to maturity in Christ. The only criterion not demanded of all believers is the ability to teach and, even then, one would hope members would grow through the word and may be able to teach in time. To put it succinctly, an elder is just a godly Christian bloke, who has been a believer a while and can teach the Bible.

Elders are fundamentally teachers. They shepherd the flock through the word. But they also lead by example. Paul called the Corinthian church to 'imitate me, as I also imitate Christ' (1 Cor. 11:1). In a similar way, elders are gifted to the church as examples for the members to follow. That is exactly what Paul encouraged the Philippians to do: 'Join in imitating me, brothers and sisters, and pay careful attention to those who live according to the example you have in us' (Phil. 3:17). It is telling that after Paul outlines the eldership criteria in Titus 1, he goes on to instruct Titus to effectively encourage the whole church to develop godly character and live out their Christian lives in such a way as to commend the gospel. The very criteria Paul insists elders must fulfil are to be emulated by all church members. So, elders are to point the church to the Scriptures, encouraging them to grow up to maturity in

---

3 Carson, D.A., 'Defining Elders', *Transcript that D.A. Carson Gave At Capitol Hill Baptist Church*, 9 Marks, 1st April 1999, accessed at https://www.9marks.org/article/defining-elders-2/, accessed on 03/09/2025

Christ and to act as godly Christian examples that the church can imitate. In turn, the members should be able to look at the elders and recognise examples of godly Christian living which they can learn from and copy. The character criteria are all part of the elder's call to teach the word. Only, they are not teaching academically, they are teaching by example so that the members can see what the word says a godly Christian life looks like in practice.

This idea of example extends beyond how elders operate in their family and private lives. It certainly includes this, but also applies to all areas of church life. There are few evangelistic churches that do not have strongly evangelistic elders. There are few welcoming churches that do not have welcoming elders. There are few churches that are seeking to raise godly children that do not have elders seeking to raise godly children. The elders are to set the example within their churches. As the elders model what it is to live out a godly Christian life, the church will begin to emulate and imitate their example.

3) Equipping the saints

Let's just revisit what Paul said to the church in Ephesus concerning pastor-teachers. Only this time, let's look at what he also goes on to say about them.

> [H]e himself gave some to be apostles, some prophets, some evangelists, some pastors and teachers, to equip the saints for the work of ministry, to build up the body of Christ, until we all reach unity in the faith and in the knowledge of God's Son, growing into maturity with a

> stature measured by Christ's fullness. Then we will no longer be little children, tossed by the waves and blown around by every wind of teaching, by human cunning with cleverness in the techniques of deceit. But speaking the truth in love, let us grow in every way into him who is the head—Christ. From him the whole body, fitted and knit together by every supporting ligament, promotes the growth of the body for building itself up in love by the proper working of each individual part. (Eph. 4:11–16)

We have already seen how these particular roles are all word-based ministries. However, it is worth noticing that the purpose of these ministries - including the pastor-teacher role - is to 'equip the saints for the work of ministry'. So, elders shepherd the church through the teaching of the word and equip the members *for* works of service. What is even more interesting is that it is not the teaching of the elders that causes the body to be built up. The elders equip the members for works of ministry, those members grow in maturity *through* their works of service, and as each part of the body does what it has been called to do, the whole body builds itself up in love. The role of elders, then, is to equip the church for works of ministry so that the church can build itself up in love by serving the needs of the fellowship.

This has two big implications for our understanding of eldership. First, if the goal is to equip believers for works of ministry, then the word-ministry of elders must be designed to build up the members so that they can serve without falling for false doctrine and human deceitfulness. We have already seen in earlier chapters that members are responsible within the church for guarding right doctrine, appointing and removing their leaders, and welcoming and disfellowshipping members. Without a sound grounding in Christian doctrine, they will not be equipped to fulfil these particular responsibilities. But the duties upon each believer extend well beyond these things. To share the gospel meaningfully and address false gospel-denying ideas, members need building up in sound teaching. To fulfil the commands of Christ, members need to be taught what Scripture actually demands of them. To not fall away when life is difficult, to press on with Jesus, to continue doing all that he calls them to do, they must rely on sound teaching. So, elders are responsible for ensuring that members are equipped for works of service through the word.

Second, if the goal is to equip the members for works of service, the ministry-by-example of the elders requires them to be involved in works of service too. It is all very well insisting that elders shepherd through the word, but we elders cannot realistically expect anybody to do what we tell them the word says they must when they don't see us elders doing it ourselves. As Jeramie Rinne puts it, 'Elders expound biblical truth and refute doctrinal error. But what if the teacher's life contradicts his teaching in glaring ways? All but the most devoted Kool-Aid drinkers stop listening. People don't have much patience for the "Do as I say, not as I do" type of teacher.'[4]

What is more, elders are aiming to equip the members for service. But you simply cannot equip people to do what you have never done or never do yourself. If you want to become an

4 Rinne, *Church Elders*, p.102

electrician, there'd be no point coming to me. I can't so much as rewire a plug let alone fit a fuse box. Not only have I got no skills to pass on, you can't even attempt to imitate what I do because you'll never see me fiddling with electrics. What you need is an electrician who will take you on as an apprentice, who will work alongside you, showing you how to do the work and guiding you as you try it yourself. In exactly the same way, how can elders expect their churches to be evangelistically minded when none of them are involved in the work of evangelism? How can churches be expected to take an interest in mission when none of the elders have any concern for mission? How can churches be active in prayer when nobody ever sees the elders prioritising prayer? You will not see an evangelistic, mission-minded church that does not have at least one evangelistic, mission-minded elder. You name it, if none of the elders are seen to model it, the church won't be doing it. If the whole goal of eldership – the reason Jesus has gifted elders to the church – is to equip the members for works of service, but our members are not being equipped and not engaging in works of service because the elders aren't doing them either, we need to seriously rethink our role.

Chapter 11:

Eldership & Calling

Many people speak about *calling to ministry*. Interestingly, such calling is almost always expressed in terms of full-time Christian ministry – often a paid pastorate – and very rarely is anyone talking about a calling to eldership. Fewer still mean a call to be an elder while happily continuing in secular employment. But if there is no distinction between elders, pastors and overseers, why do so many discern a call to 'ministry' but rarely to eldership in and of itself and almost never to be an ordinary, unsung member of a local church? This suggests that our use of calling language is deeply selective. If we are not careful, 'calling' can amount to little more than an internal desire to do something, covered in a pseudo-spiritual veneer that attempts to claim God's authority on whatever we have already decided we would quite like to do.

This kind of language has become particularly associated with pastoral ministry in the local church thanks to men such as Charles Spurgeon. In *Lectures To My Students*, he insists 'The first sign of the heavenly call is an intense, all-absorbing desire for the work.' He goes on to say:

> "Do not enter the ministry if you can help it"... If any student in this room could be content to be a newspaper editor, or a grocer, or a farmer, or a doctor, or a lawyer, or a senator, or a king, in the name of heaven and earth let him go his way... We must feel that woe is unto us if we preach not the gospel; the word of God must be unto us as fire in our bones.[1]

Similarly, D. Martyn Lloyd-Jones says that a call to gospel ministry amounts to:

> a consciousness within one's own spirit, an awareness of a kind of pressure being brought to bear upon one's spirit ... then that your mind is directed to the whole question of preaching ... This is something that happens to you; it is God dealing with you, and God acting upon you by His Spirit; it is something you become aware of rather than what you do. It is thrust upon you, it is presented to you and almost forced upon you constantly in this way.[2]

As a relatively unknown pastor, differing with such evangelical luminaries as Charles Spurgeon and Martyn Lloyd-Jones can feel

---

1 Spurgeon, C.H., *Lectures To My Students*, p.35, accessed at https://www.monergism.com/thethreshold/sdg/spurgeon/Lectures%20to%20My%20Students%20-%20Spurgeon.pdf accessed on 17/09/2025

2 Lloyd-Jones, D.M., *Preaching & Preachers*, Hodder & Stoughton, London, 1971, p.104

somewhat daunting, but neither of these men claimed infallibility, and we need to countenance that they might be wrong on occasion. I believe this issue is one such time. Ultimately, I would argue theirs is not a biblical use of the word call or the concept of calling.

The word *call* is used in two main ways in Scripture. First, it is used of the general call of the gospel. For example, Matthew 22:14 says, 'many are called, but few are chosen' (ESV). There is a general gospel call that invites people to come to the Lord Jesus. Second, *calling* can refer to the inner work of grace that effectively calls people to trust in the Lord Jesus. This use of the word *call* is seen in Romans 8:28,30: 'We know that all things work together for the good of those who love God, who are called according to his purpose ... And those he predestined, he also called; and those he called, he also justified; and those he justified, he also glorified.' In the New Testament, this second use of the word *calling* is most common. It usually refers to believers who have been called to follow Jesus.

There are a few instances of *calling* being used in connection with ministry. However, four observations seem worth making. First, every instance of *calling* in respect to ministry relates to the Apostle Paul specifically (cf. Rom. 1:1; 1 Cor. 1:1; Acts 13:2, 16:10) and, certainly in two instances and arguably in three, it concerns his calling to apostleship in particular. Given the ordinary, natural call of all the other Apostles – Jesus simply talked to them face-to-face and said 'follow me' – it isn't surprising Paul would feel the need to emphasise his calling as 'one born at the wrong time' (1 Cor. 15:8), being called as he was supernaturally. Indeed, we know Paul's apostleship was questioned by the Galatians and the Corinthians, suggesting a need to clarify that he was, indeed, called by Christ to be an Apostle.

Second, every use of the word *call* in relation to Paul involved some sort of external, supernatural occurrence. At no point is the word used to mean that Paul had an unverifiable, internal feeling that others were bound to accept. For example, Galatians 1–2 outline what happened to Paul on the road to Damascus and detail how he came to be recognised by the twelve as an Apostle. There were supernatural, external and verifiable grounds to accept this particular calling, which he references in Romans 1:1 and 1 Corinthians 1:1. Similarly, in Acts 13:1–3 we're told 'the Holy Spirit spoke'. We are given verbatim what the Holy Spirit said and shown that the whole church recognised it was the Spirit who had spoken. Either the Spirit spoke audibly to the whole church or through one of the recognised prophets mentioned in 13:1. In either case, the whole church could verify this call.

Third, however we judge these particular instances of calling in relation to Paul, it is clear this was not the normal way that believers were led into mission and ministry. It seems significant that the term *calling* is not applied to anybody else other than Paul so far as ministry is concerned. The rest of the people mentioned in the New Testament serving in ministry do not have this language of calling attached to them.

Finally, *calling* is never used of elders in the local church. We read of them being appointed, we see the church being involved in recognising their leaders, but we never see church leaders called supernaturally or insisting that they have been called by God. Indeed, the New Testament emphasises external observation of character qualifications (cf. 1 Tim. 3:1–7; Tit. 1:5–9; 1 Pet. 5:1–4). It is not a matter of someone subjectively feeling led to serve the church in this way – even through a burning desire – but by the church as a whole affirming what they can see and verifying this by natural means. Just as the church in Acts 6 looked for seven men who met particular criteria, so the church has been given the responsibility of appointing elders according to the criteria laid down in Scripture. They recognise gifting by ordinary, natural observation and in this way determine whether someone is suitable to lead the church of God. They then appoint such people to the eldership.

Given all this, I am wary of the language of *calling* when it comes to eldership and pastoral ministry. Often a wedge is put between the pastor and elders whereby a pastor must be 'called' in a way that elders are not. As we have already seen, such a distinction between these roles is biblically unwarranted; likewise, the need for an inner sense of calling to either. We can affirm that God gifts people to the church and that God grows people of character, giving them abilities with which they can serve the church. But it is for the church to recognise the gifts that God has distributed amongst his people and to determine where they will be best be put to use. As such, nobody is called because of a subjective, inner sense of calling. If we're going to use the language of calling at all, nobody is called to be an elder in the local church unless and until the local church has called them.

Nor do we have to assume that unless we have an inner-burning desire to be an elder, we are not qualified or suitable for the role. It is true that 1 Timothy 3:1 says, 'If anyone aspires to be an overseer, he desires a noble work'. Nevertheless, we have to look at what that verse actually says and take what Paul says at face value: being an elder is a good thing. That is, Paul's emphasis is not on the one who aspires to be an overseer, but on that aspiration being for a good thing. He is saying being an elder is a noble work and it is noble to aspire to noble things. He is categorically not saying, if someone desires to be an elder they are definitely cut out to be one. Nor is he saying, if someone hasn't really thought about it but a church asks them to be an elder out of the blue, they cannot possibly be qualified or called. All he is saying here is that being an elder is a good thing and aspiring to eldership is a noble aspiration. His statement has nothing to say whatsoever about qualification at this point. Indeed, Paul goes on to outline the qualifications for eldership *after* he has said this, so this is not one of the criteria itself. Of course, to be an elder, that man does ultimately have to want to do it. At some point, when the church approaches him, he needs to say *yes* and not *no*. But that desire may come after he is asked by the church. It may not be a burning desire whereby he couldn't countenance doing anything else but this; he may well be content not doing it too. But there is nothing in Scripture that suggests the need for supernatural calling to eldership, nothing that implies somebody must aspire to it before a church asks and nothing that says that if they are happy to do anything else, they are not cut out for the role.

In sum, I do not think we should base our approach to appointing elders on the calling of the Apostles, and Paul in particular. There is clearly a lot that is unique to apostleship and it is a mistake to attempt to apply this to local church eldership. Furthermore, why would we think that the burning desire of our heart is a certain call from God to ministry – which his word does not say will definitely be the case – rather than assume what Scripture clearly does say: 'the heart is more deceitful than anything else' (Jer. 17:9)? Clifford Pond puts it this way:

> A man may believe in his heart that the Lord is equipping him for ministry of some kind but until a church also believes that, he should beware of self-deception. He may not be deceived, but many men have lost their way and their families have suffered because they have come to a decision about themselves before a church has called them.[3]

This understanding of 'calling' language also has implications for how we understand the duration of eldership. There are some who would argue that, because 'God's gracious gifts and calling are irrevocable' (Rom. 11:9), they are forever a pastor or elder. Some insist, despite the view of their church that they are no longer qualified for the role, their calling means they must stay in post by God's decree. Others, having been removed from post, nevertheless wish to cling to the title because they insist they were called by God. These views might well have some legitimacy if we concede that the language of calling is rightly applied to church eldership in this way.

However, I have argued here that this language of calling is largely misapplied to eldership. As Clifford Pond writes:

3 Pond, *Only Servant*, p.59

> There is a view that says 'once a pastor, always a pastor'. A man has a 'call' and no matter whether he is actually functioning as a pastor/elder or not, he is still 'Pastor Pond'. This is a hangover from ecclesiastical traditions in which laity and clergy are separated and a 'reverend' is always a 'reverend'. I believe a man is only an elder in so far that he has been called by a church to exercise a pastoral ministry in that church, and is continuing to do so. The whole notion of a man being 'ordained' by a college apart from a local church, and then sometime later being assigned to a church or called by a church seems to me to be indefensible.[4]

Not only is the language of calling never applied to church eldership in this way, the Bible gives us no pattern of anybody being appointed to church leadership this way either. What we see is the church appointing their own elders and judging their suitability by criteria that are externally verifiable. We similarly see churches given the authority to remove their elders and determine they are no longer suitable to serve in that capacity. An elder is only an elder when they are appointed by the local church and an elder is no longer an elder when they have been removed by the local church.

None of this means churches are infallible. Churches may appoint people who should never have been appointed and they may remove those who are entirely qualified that God gifted to the church to serve as elders. Scripture doesn't suggest churches never err. But it does vest the church with the authority to appoint

4 Ibid.

and remove her own leaders and suggests the collective will of a regenerate church, in whom the Holy Spirit dwells in each of its members, is a safer basis on which to appoint and remove church leaders than the internal desire of an individual who – though no less indwelt by the Spirit – has a heart that is deceitful above all things (Jer. 17:9). It is a safeguard to the church to avoid this kind of view of calling. It is the collective view of the church as a whole to which Jesus grants sole authority concerning the appointment and removal of elders and it is very dangerous to set that aside, no matter how sincere we may be about our perceived call nor how great our desire to serve in this way may be.

Chapter 12:

Eldership Authority in Operation

In many societies, particularly in Western Europe, there is a general suspicion of authority. In the minds of many the very word conjures up thoughts of jackboots, black shirts and secret police. Even if we don't have exactly these mental images, it is hard to avoid the brute reality that people frequently misuse power. Stories abound in the press about police abusing their authority, teachers abusing the trust placed in them and politicians using their position to serve their own self-interest. So rarely do we hear stories about the excellent and benevolent administration of power and authority. Mark Dever says, 'We've become accustomed to thinking about abuse and power in the same sentence, and about authoritarianism whenever we think about authority.'[1]

This inevitably causes a problem whenever we think about authority in the church. Our minds can jump to all these negative

---

1 Dever, M., 9 *Marks of a Healthy Church (3rd Edition)*, Crossway, Wheaton, Illinois, 2013, p.231

things. But we cannot escape the fact that, as John Benton points out, 'God has put authority structures within the world – in the state, the church and the family. Church leaders *do* have an authority (under God's word). They *are* meant to influence, guide and help shape people's lives.'[2] Nevertheless, it is important for us to remember that the exercise of power and authority in the local church is pointedly unlike the structures and systems we see in the world around us.

We have already seen that the highest authority in the church, under the headship of Christ, is the congregation. The members have the authority to select and deselect their own leaders. In this sense, the elders lead under the ruling authority of the members. However, we have also seen that eldership authority is not derived from the members who elect them, but from the headship of the Lord Jesus. The elders lead with the delegated authority given to them by Jesus under the rule of the membership. But how is that authority to be exercised? What kind of authority does Jesus give to those who would lead in his name?

At the Last Supper, Luke recounts:

> Then a dispute also arose among them about who should be considered the greatest. But he said to them, 'The kings of the Gentiles lord it over them, and those who have authority over them are themselves called "Benefactors." It is not to be like that among you. On the contrary, whoever is greatest among you should

2 Benton, J., *The Balanced Pastor*, Grace Publications, London, UK, 2023, p.19

> become like the youngest, and whoever leads, like the one serving. For who is greater, the one at the table or the one serving? Isn't it the one at the table? But I am among you as the one who serves.' (Lk. 22:24–27)

This is the topsy-turvy model of authority and leadership that Jesus has established for his church. It is patently not like any of the systems and structures of authority that we see in the world. According to Jesus, the one who would be greatest, who would have authority, who would be a leader, must exercise that authority as a servant.

Whatever authority God has given to elders, we must recognise three essential things about it. First, it is delegated to them by Jesus. Elders serve under the headship of Christ. It is from him that they derive their authority and it is under his word that they exercise it. Second, elders exercise their authority under the rule of the members. We will look at exactly how this relationship should function shortly, but let's just recognise for now that elders are servants who serve the members that appoint them. It is the members who put elders into leadership and it is they who remove them where necessary. The elders exercise their authority, delegated to them from Christ, under the rule of the members. Third, eldership is servant-leadership. Members appoint elders to lead through serving. Specifically, they are appointed to serve the members who recognise their qualification to lead. The authority exercised by the elders is servant-leadership.

Given these things, it follows that there are limits on the authority of elders. If elders rule under the headship of Christ, they cannot exercise authority that Scripture does not give them. Moreover, they cannot lead the church in directions Scripture does not take them. The authority of the elders does not exceed the boundaries set by the Bible. In the end, Jesus is the highest authority in the church, he exercises his authority through his word and nobody has the right to lead in ways the word does not permit. Similarly, elders do not have the right to overrule the church membership. We will look at the particular boundaries of member authority shortly, but suffice to say the members have the authority from Christ to remove any elder they deem unsuitable. Whilst the elders are tasked to lead, the church is given the responsibility of holding their leaders to account and removing them if and when they overstep the bounds of their God-given authority. The elders are also accountable to one another. We have already seen the biblical model for plural, co-equal eldership. This means the authority of any one elder is necessarily limited by the collective will of the eldership. The pastor cannot simply overrule the other elders, but must bind himself by the shared authority of the eldership that has been delegated to them by Christ and is recognised by the church members. They are to collectively seek to serve the spiritual good of the members who elected them and no one elder can ride roughshod over any, or all of, the others.

How, then, does the authority of an eldership operate in practice? There are two spheres of operation to consider. First, how elders exercise their authority to lead within the church at large. Second, how elders individually exercise their authority on the eldership itself. We will think about these in turn.

When we think of authority within the church, Abraham Kuyper's concept of *sphere sovereignty*[3] can help us understand the relationship between the elders and church members. Whilst the concept is not without its flaws – and may not even work outside the church context – it is helpful in showing how God has delegated different spheres of authority *within* the church. Here is our diagram from chapter 7 for reference:

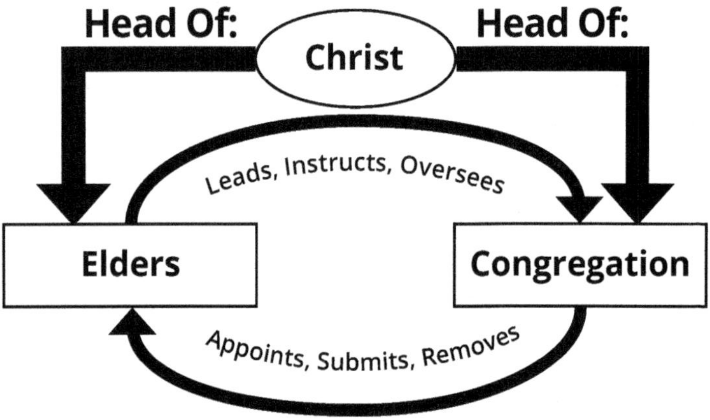

3 For an introduction to sphere sovereignty, see Kuyper, A., *Sphere Sovereignty: Church, State, Family, Education and Business*, Monergism Books, West Linn, Oregon, 2024 https://www.monergism.com/thethreshold/sdg/kuyper/Sphere%20Sovereignty-Kuyper-New.pdf accessed on 17/09/2025

We can see from the diagram that Jesus delegates specific spheres of authority to different groups within the church. The members have the authority to select their elders and then, once appointed, must submit to their authority to lead. In turn, the elders are given the right to lead, instruct and oversee the congregation. The congregation are called to submit to the authority of the elders unless and until an elder disqualifies themself either through false teaching, character failure or unrepentant sin. At this point, the members have the authority from Christ to remove an errant elder. Barring such disqualification, the members are called to submit to and obey the instruction of their elders.

Understanding these areas of responsibility and authority within the church is important for two reasons. First, it helps us avoid any sense in which the members exist to 'rein in' the elders. Members are not there to limit the ability of elders to lead. Indeed, if members are doing this, they are over-stepping the bounds of the area of responsibility God has delegated to them. Once an elder has been appointed to the eldership, the church is commanded by Jesus, through his word, to submit to their leadership and obey their instruction (cf. Heb. 13:17). It is not the role of members to keep a constant check on their elders nor to continually question every decision they take. Unless an elder has disqualified himself according to the character qualifications in Scripture, or has adopted serious theological error, the church membership must submit to his leadership. Unless the members as a whole recognise that this man's character now disqualifies him or believe that he is now teaching serious error, they are called to listen to their elders and submit to their authority. If an individual member cannot personally submit to the authority of the elders or the collective rule of the members, their only option is to find another church where they can.[4]

Second, this understanding of spheres of sovereignty within the church helps us avoid the oft-cited colour-of-the-carpet problem. As Jonathan Leeman has said, 'when congregations get caught up in these disputes about colours of the carpet or purchasing a photocopier, I think they're missing the biblical vision. Instead, we ask the leaders to train us for the work we're called to do of guarding both the gospel as well as who the gospel citizens, the gospel members of the church, are.'[5] As we noted in chapter 6 concerning the rule of church members, they are given three main areas of responsibility. These are the right to determine: who belongs to the church, what is taught in the church and who is able to lead the church. The members are to remove wayward members from membership and errant leaders from eldership. These are the spheres of responsibility that Jesus has delegated to church members. This means, beyond these spheres of authority, the members must let the elders lead. Church members' meetings

---

4 Such a step should not be taken lightly and the individual must ask serious questions about why they are sure their view is right and both the elders as a group and the majority position of the church members are wrong. The stakes are high because the person taking such a stance is likely to find these problems follow them to their new church if the issue is neither the elders nor the members but in fact insistence on their own way!

5 Leeman, J., 'Congregationalism and the Color of Your Church's Carpet', 9 *Marks*, 10th March 2018, video accessed at https://www.9marks.org/message/congregationalism-the-color-of-your-churchs-carpet/?lang=id, accessed 03/09/2025

dominated by the colour of the carpet, whether to put a new sign up outside church or any such thing are beyond the purview of what Jesus has given members to do. If the elders decide to do something that contravenes Scripture, or that evidences a problem with their character, the membership have a duty to act. But decisions about carpets, copiers and curtains hardly fall under that remit! Understanding the specific spheres of responsibility given to church members stops them from impeding elders in their God-given duty to actually lead the church.

But how does authority within the eldership operate? As we have already seen, elderships are to be co-equal and plural. That is, God's design is that more than one man should lead the local church and the authority held by each individual on the eldership is not greater than any of the others. One of the criticisms of such a position, however, is that it can lead to 'death by committee'. If no one person is charged with ultimate responsibility, how does anything actually get done? Don't churches need a linchpin? A focal point? Are pastors just passing the buck and relinquishing responsibility that they should shoulder?

Of course, if efficiency is the ultimate goal, there may be a case to be made here. But I am not convinced the Bible is so concerned about the efficiency of decision-making. Indeed, Jesus' model of servant-leadership is hardly efficient and nor is gathering a whole congregation of people to reach a decision about who to appoint as leader and who to remove from membership. But this is clearly the pattern that we are given in Scripture. Given that efficiency is not the Lord's primary concern, it shouldn't surprise us that he has instituted a model for church leadership that may not make for the most efficient decision-making process.

What is more, as much as a lack of efficiency may well be levelled at a plural-eldership-with-parity model, I would suggest that it is a far less serious concern than the dominance and abuse that more easily attend the one-man-to-rule-them-all model. Scripture is full of warnings about the reality of the human heart, and the idea that elders are immune to this is nonsense. Indeed, we even have an example in 3 John of Diotrephes – the elder who 'loves to be first' (v.9) – dominating the local church and even refusing to accept the authority and instruction of the Apostles. Many a man has been ruined by considering himself 'first amongst equals' or bishop to subordinate elders. Some are driven to mental health crises because of the weight of responsibility unduly laid upon their shoulders alone, whilst others become domineering and abusive, insisting anyone who ever criticises or raises concerns about anything in the church is 'a law unto themselves' or 'opposing God's anointed'. These things hit the Christian press with disturbing regularity. Whilst by no means a guaranteed inoculation against them, a strong eldership with co-equal authority, coupled to a membership structure that recognises the right of the membership to remove such unqualified men from leadership, makes these things less likely to take root and – where they do occur – gives the church recourse to meaningfully address them. Faced with the two models and their respective criticisms, I would take inefficiency any day of the week!

Of course, if that is the only ground on which we adopt a model, we have simply settled for pragmatism. At the end of the day, adopting the model of co-equal plural eldership with parity of esteem is not a question of finding the model which seems to avoid the worst problem. Rather, it is a question of which model most clearly reflects what we read in Scripture. After all, Christ is the head of the church and Scripture is the rule by which churches must organise themselves. As we look into it, we do not see any grounds for establishing one elder with greater authority than another (see chapter 9).

The most we can infer about authority within an eldership comes from 1 Timothy 5:17–18: 'The elders who are good leaders are to be considered worthy of double honour, especially those who work hard at preaching and teaching. For the Scripture says: Do not muzzle an ox while it is treading out the grain, and, "The worker is worthy of his wages."' That Paul is talking about proper remuneration for elders is evident from the context of v18: if 'the worker is worthy of his wages' then the one working hard at preaching and teaching must also be worthy of a stipend. This is the primary point made here. However, it is also true that there seems to be a distinction drawn between elders. Nevertheless, as we noted in chapter 7, this is not a distinction between teaching and ruling elders, but an observation that in the work of ruling and teaching some may teach more than others. At best, what we have here is a legitimate ground to call a pastor (or, full-time elder) for the purpose of devoting themselves to the teaching of the church. Such a role does not negate the co-equal authority and parity of the other elders.

In practical terms, then, an eldership will reach decisions collectively. The particular details of how they do this will vary depending on church size and the specific giftings amongst the elders. A larger church may have a wider variety of gifts and skills. A smaller church may be able to move more quickly and efficiently. A working-class church may have more trade-skills whilst a middle-class church may have more professional skills. These are all going to affect how you reach decisions as an eldership. Nevertheless, let me attempt to lay out some practical principles.

It is sensible that an elder with skills in a particular area is likely to take the lead on a relevant issue. As a matter of prudence, this simply makes sense. Why would you not utilise the skills of a builder or architect on your eldership when considering a building project? Why would you not utilise the skills of an accountant on your eldership when considering financial matters? Why would you not utilise the skills of a social worker on your eldership when considering a matter of safeguarding? It makes no sense to say, because this man has been set aside as pastor to take on the bulk of preaching and teaching, he is necessarily qualified to have greater say on any matter.

For example, my background is as a teacher and then being self-employed in the recruitment sector. This gives me absolutely no insight whatsoever into, say, employment law or financial services. The idea that because I am now a pastor, I suddenly become competent in areas in which I have no previous experience is, frankly, ridiculous. Pastors are not omni-competent. In fact, nobody is! This is the point of Paul's body metaphor for the church. So, with parity of esteem on an eldership, it makes perfect sense that those with relevant skills will take the lead on any given matter that falls within their area of expertise. Taking a lead on the issue at hand does not, however, mean that said elder can make unilateral decisions or simply force through agreement. The matter must still be agreed by the eldership collectively, but it only makes sense to recognise the different skills and abilities God has gifted to your eldership and utilise them for the good of the church he has called you to lead.

In reaching decisions, elderships will necessarily have to talk matters through. On a large eldership a specific approach to discussion might be necessary. A church with 50 elders – an eldership the size of my church's membership – is likely to have to rely on Robert's Rules of Order (or some such structure) to ensure a helpful discussion of the matter and understand the mind of the eldership collectively. By contrast, the two or three elders of a small church can easily sit down together and have a free-flowing discussion without any need for a formal vote at the end of it to discern what their collective view on the matter is. The biblical principle of plural, co-equal eldership necessitates the ability for elders to speak freely, to discuss a matter openly and to come to a collective position. There is no biblical model for exactly how to do this and there are a range of ways it might be accomplished. This is largely going to be determined by the size of your eldership and how a meaningful discussion might take place in your particular context.

Given what we have said about the responsibilities of members – particularly concerning sphere sovereignty – the biblical model of church leadership does not necessitate the membership ratifying every decision taken by the eldership. Once men have been appointed to leadership, the church is giving them license to meaningfully lead. The elders should be free to take whatever decisions they deem necessary in the life of the church without interference from church members or the fear of every minor matter generating a barrage of questions and blockages. Elders should be free to lead the church, and members would do well to let them lead the church, so long as they are not teaching error nor disqualified from leadership because of their own character failings.

However, this does not mean elders will never want to seek the mind of the church. There are issues that are so significant that it is prudent to hear what the members think before ploughing ahead. For example, there is no biblical imperative to go to the members if the elders think it appropriate to spend tens of thousands of pounds of the church's money on something. Nevertheless, when such large sums are under discussion, it seems sensible to at least present plans to the church first to gauge opinion. In reality, as free as the elders are to lead, if the members are deeply unhappy with their leadership they may well vote with their feet. It is all very well for elders to say they are leading, but if it transpires that nobody is actually following, we should question their leadership. The Bible does not specify – beyond the three areas of responsibility that we outlined earlier – what matters the elders should bring before the church. In a sense, no matter *must* come before them to be ratified, other than those concerning who belongs, who leads and what is taught. Nevertheless, wisdom suggests that seeking the mind of the church on major matters of church direction or spending is a reasonable thing to do. Elders who truly are concerned about serving the church, rather than domineering over them, will listen to what their members have to say.

I am being purposefully broad in these principles, not least because I am trying not to say more than the Bible does. Where I am giving more detail than the Bible does, I want to be clear that these things are not demanded of elders in Scripture. Rather, these are matters of wisdom. As such, they may not be appropriate in every church all of the time. As matters of wisdom, they must be worked out depending on the size and makeup of your eldership, the giftings amongst those men and the context in which you operate. All of these things must be considered when it comes to the operation of eldership authority. What is clear from Scripture, however, is that the elders' authority should be co-equal and collective.

Chapter 13:

The Qualifications for Eldership

We mentioned in an earlier chapter that the eldership criteria are, as Don Carson put it, 'remarkable for being unremarkable'. All but two of these qualifications are demanded of every believer in every church. Of the two that aren't, not a new convert (or 'novice') is clearly not where believers are supposed to stay. Taken in the round, we are looking for a godly bloke, who has been a Christian for a while, and who can teach the Bible.

Sadly, churches often end up looking for things like *charismatic personality* even though it isn't demanded by Scripture. They are quick to be impressed by those with a track record in business or who are excellent networkers. These are, of course, skills that may well be used to the glory of God in a local church. It is obviously not the case that somebody is *disqualified* from eldership as a result of these abilities. But it is important that we recognise that such abilities by themselves in no way *qualify* someone for eldership. Nor does the Bible demand them. Its focus lies elsewhere. Should a person meet the given biblical qualifications, these skills might well be useful, but it is a mistake to latch onto such things and appoint such individuals to eldership, irrespective of the qualities Jesus actually expects from leaders in his church.

One of the things Jesus does demand is an ability to teach. Naturally then, churches are frequently impressed by those who are able to teach well. That is all well and good, but many are so dazzled by this one particular skill that they pay little attention to all the other character criteria that the Bible also requires. It is hard to avoid the conclusion that many churches are more interested in skills and abilities than in garden-variety matters of character. All too often, 'useful' skills and abilities that might be turned to the advantage of the church – so that our fellowship might be 'put on the map' – take priority over the less glamorous yet vital criteria. Not to put too fine a point on it, this approach will likely end in disaster. Scandal after scandal in the modern church can be traced back to two often related problems: (1) lack of accountable church structures; and (2) lack of qualifying character. We play down these matters of character at our peril. Which begs the question, what does the Bible actually require to qualify as a church elder?

Character criteria

There are two main passages of Scripture that lay out the qualifications for eldership. They are 1 Timothy 3:2–7 and Titus 1:6–9. I will briefly survey the criteria set out in these passages:

1) Above Reproach/Blameless (1 Tim. 3:2; Tit. 1:6)

This qualification does not mean that an elder is without sin. 1 John 1:8–9 tells us nobody would meet such a qualification. Nor does this mean that an elder will never be accused of anything (cf. 1 Pet. 3:16). Rather, an elder is to be regarded as a man of integrity with the kind of character that makes any accusation against him seem more unlikely than not on first hearing (cf. Acts 25:7).

2) The husband of one wife (1 Tim. 3:2; Tit. 1:6)

The Greek, word-for-word, reads as *one woman man* or *one wife husband.* The qualification is most likely designed to disqualify those in polygamous relationships. But it also affirms a man as qualified if he has a good track record of monogamous marital faithfulness. Almost all agree that this qualification does not rule out a man who has re-married after the death of a first wife. Also, taking the words at face value, and given there are biblically legitimate grounds to do so under certain circumstances, it is unlikely this automatically rules out someone re-married after a divorce.

3) Sensible/Temperate/Sober-minded (1 Tim. 3:2)

Depending on the Bible version you read, the Greek word *nēphalios* gets translated as *sober*, *temperate*, *sober-minded*, *sensible* or *vigilant*. Certainly, a sense of being *sober* does lie behind the word. The question is whether this should be understood in a literal sense relating to drunkenness or more figuratively to being sober-minded or sensible. Given other explicit qualifications on drunkenness and self-control, a figurative understanding seems preferrable. *Sensible* carries the helpful double-meaning of being in control of one's senses (that is, sober in a literal sense) and, at the same time, having good sense and judgement. This qualification is describing somebody whose general decision-making is not erratic or inscrutable, but a person who makes sensible choices and reasonable judgements in the ordinary run of things.

4) Self-controlled (1 Tim. 3:2; Tit. 1:8)

An elder in the church must be characterised by self-control. Do they control their emotions and behaviours? This doesn't mean being emotional disqualifies someone. A man is only disqualified if his emotions – whichever they may be – are out of control and rule over him in ways that mean he does not control how he behaves. Similarly, it rules out those in the grip of addictions. Whilst many recognise this in relation to alcohol, drugs and pornography, the likes of caffeine and eating addictions can be too easily overlooked because they are more culturally acceptable and easily hidden in certain circles. The qualification is not about tendencies to one thing or another, or even partaking of particular things, but whether a man seeks to control his emotions and behaviour or whether he is ruled by them.

5) Respectable (1 Tim. 3:2)

As with almost all these qualifications, being respectable will be to some degree culturally defined. An elder will not be characterised by flouting the accepted standards of their community. They will not be considered disreputable and unworthy of respect because of their behaviour.

6) Hospitable (1 Tim. 3:2; Tit. 1:8)

Being hospitable is not unique to elders; it is expected of all believers (cf. Rom. 12:13; Heb. 13:2; 1 Pet. 4:9; 2 Tim. 1:16). Hospitality is about making people feel welcome and receiving them generously. In view is a hospitable spirit. Whilst refusing to have people in your home may evidence an unwillingness to offer hospitality, having guests in your house is not the primary or only outlet. This qualification is concerned with welcoming and generously receiving others in such a way as makes clear they are important to you, whether this takes place in the church building, your house or out in the community. The home may be a significant tool for hospitality, but it isn't the only means of showing hospitality nor evidencing a hospitable spirit.

7) Able to teach/Holding to the faithful message as taught (1 Tim. 3:2; Tit. 1:9)

Amongst the character criteria, this is the only skill or ability demanded of elders. There is nothing here that insists an elder must be an able preacher nor even that they must be able to teach publicly. Specifically, Titus 1:9 states an elder must be able to encourage with sound teaching and refute those who contradict it. This means, at a minimum, an elder must be able to encourage someone privately from Scripture, recognise when people are teaching error and be able to refute them with the Scriptures.

8) Not an excessive drinker (1 Tim. 3:3; Tit. 1:7)

This qualification rules out those who regularly get drunk. The ESV helpfully translates it as 'not a drunkard'. There is no ban on drinking here – otherwise Jesus himself would be disqualified from eldership in his own church – nor does it put any specific limits on the amount or number of times one might drink. Neither is the qualification directly concerned with alcoholism, as that is covered by the earlier qualification of self-control, which rules out those under addiction. Rather, this disqualifies anyone who, whilst not an alcoholic addicted to drinking, nevertheless regularly gets drunk.

9) Not a bully but gentle (1 Tim. 3:3; Tit. 1:7)

'Not a bully' is a helpful translation because physical violence is not the only thing in view. An elder should not be someone who batters people with either their fists or their words. They are not to threaten others. Instead, they will be gentle and patient, not easily angered.

10) Not quarrelsome (1 Tim. 3:3)

This cannot mean that the man never disputes anything with anyone because Titus 1:9 makes clear there are times elders need to refute people. Rather, this is concerned with not picking pointless fights and arguments. An elder should not be characterised by a hyper-critical spirit that takes everyone to task. Nor should they be constantly starting arguments with people. Elders will inevitably have to address issues in the church, often directly. Plenty of issues will arise without the elders searching them out, but elders ought not to be the cause of those arguments. Rather, an elder ought to have the wisdom to know whether a matter needs addressing or can be left alone.

11) Not greedy for money (1 Tim. 3:3; Tit. 1:7)

Jesus was clear that you cannot serve God and money (cf. Mt. 6:24). He was also clear that the Pharisees – whom he frequently called *hypocrites* – were lovers of money (cf. Lk. 16:14). Jesus says those who would lead his church are not to be like this. We must be clear that this does not rule out those who *have* money nor is it wrong to generously support an elder. In fact, Scripture says elders are worthy of double honour and cites workers being worthy of their wages (cf. 1 Tim. 5:17–18). But an elder should not be serving in the church in order to line his own pockets nor should he be someone who can easily be swayed by money. Anyone who is greedy for money is not qualified to be a leader in the church of God.

12) Manages his household competently (1 Tim. 3:4–5)

There is a link between family responsibilities and church responsibilities. Paul asks, 'If anyone does not know how to manage his own household, how will he take care of God's church?' If a man cannot manage his household duties, budget and family responsibilities, there is little evidence that he will be able to manage any of these things in the church. If a man is unable or unwilling to care for his own family and household, he is unlikely to be able or willing to properly care for the household of God. An elder must manage his home well.

13) Faithful children/children under control (1 Tim. 3:4; Tit. 1:6)

Closely related to good household management is having 'faithful children'. The Greek word *pistos* has been the cause of some translation headaches because it can be rendered either *faithful* or *believing*. So, are elders supposed to have faithful children or children that are believers? The context suggests the former. Specifically, Titus 1:6 insists on faithful children 'who are not accused of wildness or rebellion.' Similarly, 1 Timothy 3:4 says an elder must 'have his children under control with all dignity.' Further, 1 Timothy 3:4 speaks about managing the *household*. This suggests the matter at hand is those living in the family home under the authority of the head of the household. However we translate the word *pistos*, it seems clear that insubordinate children and parents who do not treat their children with dignity are the disqualifying matters here. An elder will have children who submit to his authority and are not insubordinate or wild. They will submit to their father, not from fear, but because of the dignity with which he treats them. The inference is that if a man is able to command the respect of his family in this way, he is also likely to gain the willing submission of church members because of the dignity with which he will treat them.

14) Not a new convert (1 Tim. 3:6)

An elder must not be a new believer. The reason for this qualification is in the same verse. Making someone an elder too early may make him puffed up and conceited. Elders are to be mature members of the church, with a track record of walking faithfully with Christ. They cannot credibly act as an example to the flock without it.

15) A good reputation among outsiders (1 Tim. 3:7)

Like being 'above reproach', this does not mean that everyone outside the church is always happy with this elder nor that accusations are never fired. Rather, there should be nothing in the life of this elder that would bring the gospel into disrepute within the community. Generally, people should think well of him and have no reason to consider his behaviour or lifestyle to be incompatible with the gospel he proclaims. Of particular concern is anything that would cause unbelievers in the community to blaspheme the name of Christ because of the behaviour of a leader in his church.

16) Not arrogant (Tit. 1:7)

Elders in the church are not to be arrogant and full of themselves. The reason new converts are not to be appointed is because doing so may well lead them into this very sin. Instead, as Jesus commanded, the one who would be considered first must be last, the one who would be great must make himself least. As elders are called to be servants, they cannot be those with an overly high opinion of themselves. Interestingly, this characteristic is often discovered when a church asks a man to wait before becoming an elder or tells him he may not be suitable at the current time. His reaction can show whether he is an arrogant sort or someone who humbly accepts the church's judgement.

17) Not hot-tempered (Tit. 1:7)

This is not exactly the same as the earlier qualification about bullying. It is an outworking of the qualification to be self-controlled.

An elder should not be a man prone to regular outbursts of anger. His temper must be kept in check.

18) A lover of good (Tit. 1:8)

In short, if God calls something good, an elder will love that thing too. His desires will increasingly be conforming to Christ's, and he will recognise and enjoy what God calls good.

19) Righteous (Tit. 1:8)

It seems unlikely that these qualifications are merely referring to the fact that the elder has been made perfectly righteous and holy in Christ, which is true of every Christian. Rather, the word translated *righteous* may better be understood as *upright* or *acts righteously*. So, an elder should have integrity in their dealings with people. They should be honest, fair and faithful.

20) Holy (Tit. 1:8)

The word translated *holy* (Gk., *hosios*) refers to living a life that is pleasing to God. An elder is an example of a believer who is living in such a way that they reflect the holiness to which they have been called.

There are three things worth underlining about these qualifications for eldership. First, all of these things, except being able to teach, are demanded of all believers. So, we mustn't overstate what is being asked of elders here. Elders are qualified if they are godly examples of what all Christians are called to be, along with being able to teach the Bible.

Second, most of these criteria will be culturally and contextually defined. A man may be viewed as qualified in one context and yet, in another, appear not to meet some of the requirements due to cultural expectation. For example, treating your children with dignity will look different in different contexts. What if one culture considers it dignified to smack your children and weak parenting not to do it while another says smacking your children is abusive parenting and your local reputation will be ruined if you do? Similarly, what constitutes a new convert? In one setting, the whole church may consist of fifth-generation Christians who themselves have been believers for decades. Another setting might be full of people who have all been believers less than five years. Furthermore, a man qualified to be an elder in one church may not be suitable in another because of how these criteria are discerned differently across cultures and contexts. To give an obvious example, someone might be able to teach in France but unable in Finland because they can speak one language and not the other. This qualifies them as an elder in one place but not in another.

Finally, these two passages are not giving a comprehensive and complete 'job description' of eldership. This becomes obvious when we think about various things Paul has not mentioned but that clearly make somebody incapable of leading a local church. As mentioned above, being able to speak the same language is not a criterion Paul lists but it is necessary for somebody to effectively lead the church. There are things we can legitimately demand of elders that are not explicit in Scripture. However, we have to ensure that any extra-biblical requirement is a culturally or contextually appropriate outworking of the biblical criteria.

I am convinced the tendency of some to create extra-biblical criteria lies behind the inability of many to find elders within their membership. It is not that their people are unqualified, but that criteria have been added that the Lord does not demand. Of course, we must think about the implications of the biblical criteria within our particular communities. Of course, being respectable on a council estate in Northern England might look different to respectability in a middle-class suburb in the South of England. We would be wise to define what respectability in our particular context looks like in practice and then measure potential elders against such standards. However, we have to make sure that when we insist on what is not explicitly mentioned in Scripture, we are only asking elders to meet the culturally appropriate outworking of explicitly required biblical criteria.

Let me expand on my previous example to show what this might look like. In working-class communities it is acceptable and not at all unkind to engage in banter. In middle-class communities, this can come across to some as aggressive or even bullying. In one community, banter is actively hospitable – a good qualification for eldership – whereas in another it is not considered gentle and may even be disrespectful, potentially disqualifying a man from eldership. This may qualify a man in one place but not in another if he is unable to adapt culturally. So, it is legitimate to require what is not expressly stated in Scripture so long as it is a genuinely contextual outworking of what the Bible does ask of elders.

Chapter 14:

The Process of Appointing Elders

We have already seen that it is a church responsibility – the role of the membership as a whole – to appoint their elders. But how exactly are churches supposed to go about doing this?

In the first instance, there needs to be proper spiritual preparation. When Jesus was going to appoint the Twelve, he spent all night praying (Lk. 6:12–16). Similarly, when the church in Antioch were moved by the Spirit to set apart Paul and Barnabas – even though they had word from God to do so – they spent time in prayer before setting them apart (Acts 13:1–3). The bottom line is: appointing elders is a spiritual business. The appointment of a new elder is not a matter of picking your mates, or whoever seems to have the most charismatic ability; it is a matter of recognising spiritual gifting. If God gifts elders to the local church, and members are tasked with the job of recognising those who have been gifted to them, it follows that the church should be seeking God's will in the matter. It is foolish to press ahead in appointing an elder without first praying that God would make clear to the church who he has gifted to them for eldership.

The church must also assess whether a man has the qualifications, attributes and gifting according to the criteria laid down in the word. It is not a matter of saying 'I really like this man' or 'I get on well with him'. We have to set aside emotive arguments and personal prejudice and properly assess the person before us in light of what God's word actually requires of him. So, the church members must prepare by familiarising themselves with the biblical criteria for eldership. This is why, before appointing an elder, the church must give itself to the reading of the word and prayer.

The church must pray that they would be spiritually discerning and understand what the word is asking them to discern. They must pray that they would honestly assess the men before them according to what Scripture demands. They must pray for personal understanding. They must pray that God would judge the thoughts and intentions of their hearts, that they would set aside anything that would inhibit right judgement. The members should be thinking about where the church is lacking and pray that God would raise up suitable men with appropriate gifts to fill the void. They should pray that God would make clear to them when such a person has been gifted to the church. They should pray they will be able to discern not only God's will but the gifts God has distributed amongst them. First and foremost, when it comes to appointing elders, a church must prepare themselves spiritually. They prepare by acquainting themselves with the scriptural criteria and by praying for God to grant them the gifts necessary for the role and for the discernment to recognise when he has given them to the church.

Though church members must be suitably prepared to appoint elders, there needs to be a clear process for doing so. We have already seen that the approach to appointing a new Apostle (Acts 1) and then choosing the seven (Acts 6) involved the whole congregation. Particularly, in Acts 6, it was notably the congregation who were themselves to choose seven men to serve. Their choice was then ratified by the Apostles, who formally appointed them. We noted in chapter 6 that the Greek verb used in Acts 14:23 for the term *appointed* (*cheirotonēsantes*) literally means 'stretch out the hand' and was a term used for voting. It is clear then that the church must be actively involved in the process of choosing its own leaders. More specifically, the church must be involved in the appointment of elders.

It also bears saying, however, that elders must be able to work together. It is all very well for the church to want a particular man as an elder, but if it is clear to the other elders that they will not be able to work together the appointment is not a wise one. There are biblical grounds for this. At the end of Acts 15, Paul and Barnabas discuss returning to the churches they have planted to see how they are doing, but they disagree over whether to take John Mark. Paul, arguing from past experience working with John Mark, does not think they will be able to work together. John Mark had abandoned them previously and Paul does not want a repeat performance. We're told that Paul and Barnabas 'had such a sharp disagreement that they parted company' (v.39). Paul ended up partnering with Silas whilst Barnabas and John Mark went to Cyprus. Whatever else we may want to take from this episode, it seems there are biblical grounds to say those who will have to work together have the freedom to determine whether an appointment is appropriate. If Paul can reject John Mark because of concerns over his reliability, and Jesus himself says in Matthew 12:25 'Every kingdom divided against itself is headed for destruction, and no city or house divided against itself will stand', it seems prudent – and biblically legitimate – for serving elders to recognise whether they can work with a candidate for eldership.

The question is, how do we synthesise this legitimate ground for elders to determine whether they can work together with the responsibility for choosing leaders being given to the whole church? It makes sense that the church must be involved in the process because they will ultimately be asked to submit to the authority of those appointed. Clifford Pond says, 'people are much more likely to respect one in whose appointment they have had some part than one foisted on them with little or no consultation.'[1] It similarly makes sense that the elders themselves must be involved in the process because they will have to submit to one another and work together on the eldership. Not having adequate involvement from elders 'is the highroad to chaos and in the past has been one of the prime causes of churches losing their theological moorings.'[2] Nevertheless, the Bible does not give a specific blow-by-blow process for appointing elders. We have only these principles: (1) the whole church must be involved; (2) it is ultimately the church's responsibility to choose its own leaders; (3) the elders must be able to work together.

1 Pond, *Only Servants*, p.83

2 Ibid.

Given that there is no specific process laid down in Scripture, there is a level of flexibility that allows different churches to come up with appropriate processes depending on their context and situation. The process I am going to describe is consistent with the biblical principles that we have outlined. However, I recognise it is not explicitly what Scripture says *must* happen and so there is room for doing things another way. This is my suggestion for how to harmonise these biblical principles. I am drawing on both good and bad examples from my own experience to outline what seems to me to be a wise process.

In line with the biblical principles already outlined, and after the church have been spiritually prepared, the first step is to identify suitable candidates for eldership. Given that it is good to utilise every gift God has given to the church – including teaching and leadership gifts – the church should not automatically look outside the congregation for new leaders. It is good to look internally first and assess whether any suitable elders exist within the congregation. With that said, if there are none, it is perfectly legitimate to search for elders externally. Just as Barnabas was sent from the church in Jerusalem to help lead in Antioch, and he found Saul and took him there to help also, there are biblical grounds for churches to gift workers to other places and for receiving churches to utilise them in leadership. Though it is good to look internally first, there is no biblical reason not to welcome an elder from outside.

Given the necessity for the whole church to be involved in the process, it should be open for all members of the church to suggest suitable candidates. Nevertheless, because the existing elders must be able to work with any newly appointed man, recognising potential elders can happen in one of two ways. First, the elders may propose a candidate to the church, someone they recognise as biblically qualified with whom they would be able to work. Such a candidate could only be appointed if the church members accept the elders' recommendation and can affirm that they also recognise this man to be suitable. Alternatively, members of the church may propose a potential elder. Given the need for eldership involvement, it makes sense for the recommendation to come from the member to the elders in the first instance. There is no point approaching the person or putting the question to the members if the elders know they will not be able to work with this person and the recommendation is therefore not appropriate. However, if the elders agree that the candidate is suitable and they can work together, the elders should make that recommendation to the church. Again, the candidate would only be appointed if the church as a whole agrees. This two-fold approach to recognising who might be a suitable elder maintains the need for both elders and members to be involved in the process. It also gives the elders a say on suitability while leaving the final decision in the hands of the church as a whole.

Once suitable candidates have been identified, how should the mind of the church be discerned? As argued earlier, I believe that elder-led, member-ruled congregationalism is the most biblically faithful form of church governance. Within such a model, it makes sense for elders to make proposals – that is to lead on the matter – whilst final authority is given to the church members to decide. The question is, how do you discern what the elders and members think respectively?

Understanding the mind of the elders is fairly straightforward. Ultimately, they must talk about it and agree amongst themselves. Some would argue that a majority position among the elders is not enough for a candidate to be recommended. The smaller your eldership, the truer that may be. There is a good case to be made that if any of the elders do not think a candidate suitable, the appointment should not go forward. The reasoning behind this is that it is difficult to work together if you know that some never considered you suitable. If you did not consider the person suitable, it is difficult to submit yourself to them on the eldership when you don't really think they should be there at all. Where there is a disagreement, it is all too easy to overrule with a hand-waving reference to the person not really being a suitable elder. This is a matter of wisdom and is not a specific biblical requirement but I think there is real sense in ensuring all the elders are on board before appointing a candidate. In terms of a recommendation, however, this means if the elders are proposing a candidate, it is clear this is something agreed upon by all the elders.

Discerning the mind of the church is a slightly different matter. If we hold to the earlier understanding of the Greek verb *cheirotonēsantes* (translated: *appointed*) to mean literally 'stretch out the hand' or 'to vote', it is reasonable to discern the mind of the members through a formal vote. The larger your congregation, the more likely it is to need a formal means of discerning the views of the church. In a smaller congregation, it is easier to have more intimate discussion in church members' meetings. Whilst there is wisdom in the elders hearing from the members before any vote is taken, allowing people room to formally express themselves in a members' meeting so that nothing is done behind closed doors is important. Much damage has been done by appearing to keep things secret. If elders set themselves up as the ones who will present the views of the church as they seek consensus, they become open to the charge of swinging the vote. Whilst members may not know what everyone else thinks, often they will have a sense about it (rightly or wrongly). A formal vote, done publicly in a members meeting, leaves no room for anyone to doubt the mind of anybody else.

At a minimum, the church must look for a majority of members to vote in favour of the elders' recommendation. However, I would argue it is prudent to seek a super-majority when it comes to appointing new elders. Some find a consensus model appealing – that is, only moving forward with 100% agreement of the church membership – but this comes with several problems. Whilst efficiency is not our ultimate goal, at some point decisions need to be taken and waiting for absolute consensus can stymy any possibility of reaching one. If 99% of the church agree, but one member demurs, the whole process is stuck. This can lead the one with genuine concerns over an appointment to feel pressured into agreeing to what they firmly believe is not right so as not to be seen as holding the church to ransom. By contrast, others may be more than happy to hold the church to ransom and take great pleasure in the full exercise of their powers. Ironically, this model causes exactly the same problem as the one-man-to-rule-them-all model of ministry. It ultimately places all power in the hands of one member if they choose to dissent from the majority. Member rule is collective but the consensus model allows a tiny minority to overrule the majority of members to whom authority has ultimately been given. For these reasons, I believe a consensus model, whilst at first blush seeming to have a high view of the members' authority, in practice actively undermines God-given member rule.

At the same time, a slim-majority of 51% is not a strong basis for expecting the church to submit to someone's leadership. Elders will at some point inevitably have to take decisions that are unpopular. It is far easier to do so, and more straightforward for the church to submit, when an overwhelming majority of members have recognised their suitability to lead. It is also true that some elders will inevitably have their critics. If, however, nearly 50% of the church did not think they were a suitable candidate for eldership, the chances of having a lot of critics and much dissent becomes considerably higher. Such a slim majority is a poor basis for leadership. Therefore, a super-majority seems preferable. It ensures a sizeable majority of the church, along with the elders, recognise this individual is suitable to lead, but avoids the issue of the whole church being held hostage by one or two individuals. There is no biblical insistence upon a super-majority, but it seems sensible to require one.

Given the need for broad agreement amongst the elders and the members, adequate time must be built into the process to allow for the church to have conversations with potential candidates. Again, there is no biblical mandate for a set period of time to give people. However, the elders will almost certainly have been having conversations with one another for a time before agreeing to make a recommendation. It seems right, then, to give the members fair warning and allow them time to talk with the candidate(s) too.

Even when you appoint internally and people know the candidate already, they may not have been considering them in terms of eldership suitability until a recommendation is made. It is one thing to generally see a person as a good member who serves well, a generally nice person to have around, but it is another thing altogether to assess a person as a suitable elder. However long we may deem suitable, the church must be given a reasonable amount of time to think, assess and speak to a person being recommended in light of what they are going to be asked to do. A recommendation should be made by the elders followed by a suitable amount of time for the church to consider the recommendation. This also provides an opportunity for members to speak to the elders directly about any concerns they may have. A members' meeting should be called where a frank and open discussion can take place before a final vote is taken on the matter.

If the elders' recommendation is accepted by a super-majority of church members, the candidate should be informed that they have been accepted onto the eldership. They should then be formally recognised as an elder of the church; this is probably best done at a Sunday meeting. This informs both church members and the wider congregation that this man is now a leader in this local church.

The following flowchart summarises the process outlined in this chapter:

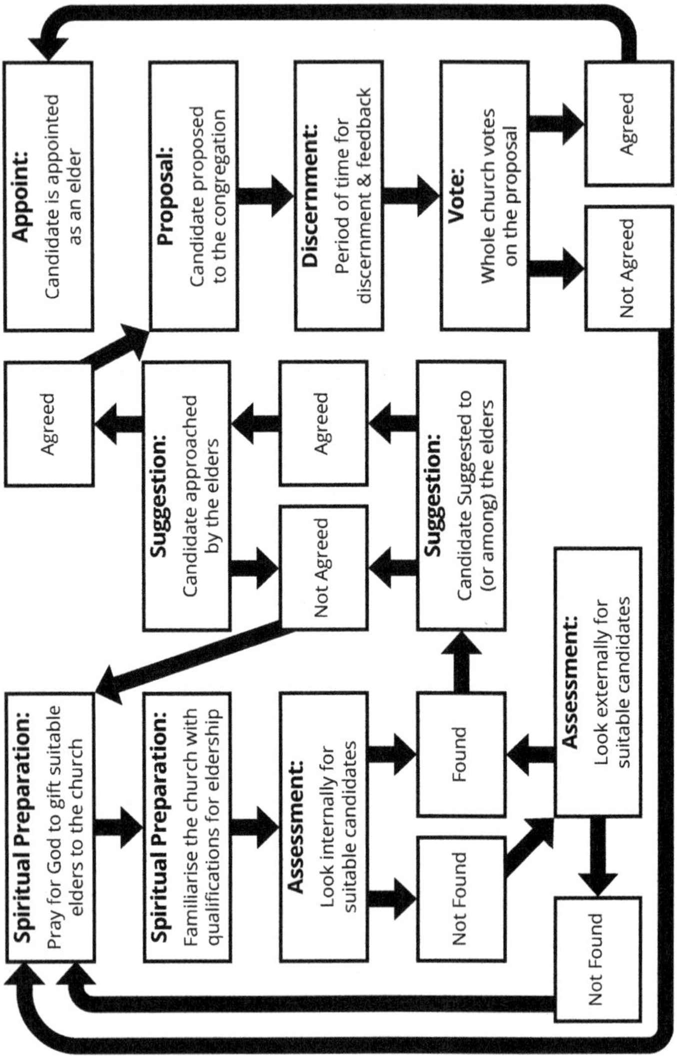
Spiritual Preparation:
Pray for God to gift suitable elders to the church
Spiritual Preparation:
Familiarise the church with qualifications for eldership
Assessment:
Look internally for suitable candidates
Not Found
Found
Assessment:
Look externally for suitable candidates
Not Found
Suggestion:
Candidate Suggested to (or among) the elders
Not Agreed
Agreed
Suggestion:
Candidate approached by the elders
Agreed
Proposal:
Candidate proposed to the congregation
Discernment:
Period of time for discernment & feedback
Vote:
Whole church votes on the proposal
Not Agreed
Agreed
Appoint:
Candidate is appointed as an elder

Chapter 15:

The Relationship of Elders with Other Elders

In a family there are different relationships. There is the relationship between husband and wife, between parents and children, and from sibling to sibling. We know these different relationships do not operate in the same way. A husband should not be treating his wife like his daughter. A sister should not be treating her brother like her father. These things are pretty obvious and they apply as much to relationships in the household of God as they do in the family home.

In the following few chapters, I want to sketch out the different relationships an elder will have within the church. In particular, how should an elder relate to the different people who impact their ministry? In this chapter, we will think about the relationship of elders with other elders.

Leading by relational example

As we have seen, plural eldership is the model to which all churches ought to aspire. A church without a plurality of elders, whilst able to function and not illegitimate, is nevertheless deficient. This deficiency will not only be seen in the life of the church, but will take a toll on any lone pastor. The principle of plural eldership is not only for the church's benefit, but for the benefit of those who are called to lead.

One of the ways elders are called to lead in the church is through example. One of the examples the elders ought to set is in their relationships. The church members should be able to look at the relationships between the elders and see, to some extent, how their relationships with one another ought to function too. Just as telling the members to do evangelism when the elders don't do any is likely to ring hollow, so calling the members to live out particular relationships in the church is going to be difficult if they don't see the elders doing the same. The members must be able to see the relational life of the elders as an example to them of the kind of relationships Jesus calls them to have together.

Contrary to some popular teaching, I don't think this means elders must be best buddies. Don't mishear me here. If elders are at each other's throats, they will hardly thrive and if they hate one another, not only are they disqualified from eldership, they disqualify themselves from membership of the church (cf. 1 Jn. 4:20–21). But many believe unless the elders are best friends, and carefully cultivate that sort of relationship together, they will not survive; the eldership will break down and the church will follow their example and have no love for one another. I have known some put such a high level of store by this idea that *unless* you are best friends, they reckon your leadership to be inadequate, unbiblical and ultimately damaging to the church. Frankly, that is nonsense. Ironically, by putting such pressure on developing that sort of relationship – just as children in the playground soon find out – this is the very means by which you guarantee friendship will not blossom. Forcing someone to be your best friend is rarely a good way to gain a best friend.

When I say you don't need to be best friends, that is exactly what I mean. Elders are called to love one another just as you would love any other brother or sister in Christ. Elders must be able to work together in the ministry that Jesus has given them, as you would in any area of ministry working with other believers. Elders are called to be an example to the flock and so must live out what Scripture calls all members of the church to do. But if we don't think everyone in the church must be best friends with everyone else – even though they are rightly and genuinely to love and serve one another – there is no reason to assume elders must be best friends or provide this sort of example to the membership. In fact, it sets an even better and more important example when we *are not* necessarily best friends. That is, we showcase the importance of loving and serving together irrespective of how we judge our friendship. Being very different people – in age, stage, personality and interest – and yet still loving one another and working together for the cause of the gospel, being clearly united in purpose and desire for the glory of Christ, sets an even more compelling example to the flock than the juvenile 'best friends' demand of some. Of course, if you happen to be best friends with folks on your eldership, that's lovely. Praise God! It just bears saying: this isn't, of itself, a biblical requirement nor a matter vital to the health of the local church.

Parity in practice

We have already seen that elders ought to have parity of esteem. That is, no one elder should be considered above the others or have a greater say. This means elders must be willing to listen well to their fellow elders. They must also be ready to recognise where another elder carries more authority than they do. I don't mean that one elder might have a greater say or a more powerful vote. Rather, for example: if I have no skills whatsoever when it comes to budgeting – but another elder happens to be a chartered accountant – more weight should be placed on the views and opinions of the one with greater expertise. Different elders are likely to take a lead in different areas based on the respective skills and abilities God has gifted them. In this sense, there should never be one 'lead elder' so much as a genuine team of elders on which different men at different times take a natural lead given their backgrounds, skills and abilities. None of this means that all the other elders are duty bound to do exactly what the more expert elder says on the matter; just that they should humbly recognise where someone else has greater knowledge and skills and, therefore, weigh their views and opinions accordingly.

In light of this, it makes sense for the eldership to be made up of men from a variety of backgrounds. It is good, so far as it is possible, for the eldership to represent a reasonable cross-section of the church. It is good for men with different temperaments, skills and backgrounds to work together. It is good to have a mix of people with different political views on the eldership. All these things limit cultural blind spots that might not be noticed by a more homogenous group and give a breadth of experience, backgrounds, skills and knowledge that expresses the unity in diversity to which Christ calls his church. It allows the elders to demonstrate the humble listening and learning from one another, for the sake of the kingdom, that ought to happen amongst the members in other areas of ministry. It makes the relational life of the elders better because they must learn to live with and hear challenge and encouragement from those who may see the world differently. It gives opportunities for the church to see the kind of giving and receiving of encouragement, challenge and rebuke that ought to be commonplace amongst God's people.

Protection

One of the issues with the 'best friends' approach to church leadership is that it makes it very difficult for members to hold their elders to account. It is a big enough thing to raise concerns at all, but to only be able to do so with somebody's best friend feels like the matter will be prejudiced even before you begin. This model makes it very hard to be assured that an eldership will investigate matters fairly and for the church to really see that the elders are not there to protect one another, but ultimately to protect the church. However, if we have an eldership from a range of backgrounds, with genuine parity established between them – and the church see a willingness amongst them to submit to one another, to encourage and love each other, as well as challenge and rebuke where needed –

church members will have greater confidence in the investigations undertaken by elders where required.

If an accusation is made against an elder, the other elders have a duty to properly investigate, without prejudice, so that the church can have confidence that the elders really are there to protect them. However, if there is no evidence that warrants action, the elders have a duty to protect the reputation of the accused elder. Indeed, serious accusations in the church cannot have a neutral outcome. Either an elder is in sin, disqualified from eldership and must be removed when compelling evidence is brought to light, or someone is bringing false accusations against an elder and must be removed from the church for seeking to slander and tarnish their reputation. All too often, churches either fail to investigate their elders and cannot fathom that their leaders would ever do such things, or else accusations are simply believed, actioned and – if later proven untrue – carry no consequence for those seeking to damage a servant in the church of Christ. The relationship between elders should be close enough that they can investigate these things meaningfully whilst not so chummy that nobody will have any confidence that wrongdoing will be appropriately dealt with. If elders are to be just – and seen to be acting in the interests of the church – elders in sin must be removed from ministry, whilst members making false accusations must similarly be removed from the church.

More positively, a plurality of elders – with a close but not necessarily 'best friends' relationship – can help each other to continue walking faithfully with Christ. Elders are to watch out for the spiritual state of their fellow elders. They are to encourage one another to press on in Christ and continue pursuing holiness. They are to rebuke and challenge one another when they begin to wander from faithfulness to Jesus. In church leadership, pride is never far away. A belief that we lead because we are better than others, a belief that our abilities are necessary for the church to thrive, a belief that God is working because of something about us – these things easily creep into our thinking. The relationship between the elders must be such that others can see and challenge these things when they arise.

A relationship of openness and prayer

The relationship between elders should be one characterised by openness and prayer. If we are to keep watch over one another's souls, we must be willing to be open. That is, to share about our struggles, our burdens and our besetting sins. We must be willing to let other elders hold us to account on these things. Not least, if we want our members to be open with us, we can hardly refuse to be open with one another. Nobody will be open if they fear our judgement and few will share with us if we are never known to share with anyone else.

But it is not just a matter of sharing. Elders ought to be praying for one another. It is very easy in weekly elders' meetings to just get caught up in all the business – after all, elders are called to lead the church – but we mustn't neglect prayer. So, in the elders' meetings at Oldham Bethel Church, we have chosen to split the meeting into two halves. The first half focuses on people: we think about membership issues and personal matters amongst the members that we need to be aware of; we think about regular attendees who aren't yet in membership and how we might help them move towards it; we keep a watch on visitors and whether they come back. The second half focuses on more practical matters of direction and anything else to do with the running of the church. But in between these two sections, we stop and share with one another and we pray. The question is often asked, who pastors the pastors? The answer is, we pastor one another. So, each week, we share items for prayer; we share what is happening in our families; we share what is concerning and troubling us. Then, halfway through our elders meeting – between thinking about the personal needs of everyone else and the practical matters of running the church – we pray for each other.

I don't pretend ours is the perfect model, but however you do it, your eldership should be characterised by an openness in sharing and a willingness to pray for one another. It is a sign of an unhealthy eldership that refuses to be open with one another about their struggles, whether practical or personal. When your elders do not share with one another nor pray for each other, it is a sign of a legalistic judgemental culture that encourages masking and hypocrisy rather than honesty and grace. Your fellow elders will only open up, just like the rest of the church, when they are safe in the knowledge that you too will share your struggles and there is no sense of ungracious judgement. If we are to model by example to our church, and we teach our people that all of us who trust in Christ are sinners saved by grace, what do we actually convey when we never seem to admit our sin, to repent, to share openly and honestly about it? We can lead by example by being open and honest within our eldership and praying meaningfully for one another.

Disagreement is not sinful; it is inevitable and healthy

If we are characterised by openness, we are bound to find that we disagree with one another. Not only is disagreement not sinful, it is inevitable. More to the point, disagreement is a sign of a healthy eldership.

On any number of subjects, elders will have different judgements. Within our own eldership we have had disagreements about the order of service, the candidates for baptism, how to word job adverts for new workers, to name just a few issues. There is nothing sinful about any of these disagreements. Any one of us might be in sin if we were disagreeing in such a way as to denigrate our fellow elders or if we were doing so for self-serving, ungodly reasons. However, I don't think generally when other elders disagree with me either thing is happening. They simply have a different judgement on a particular matter to me. The solution, in most cases, is together to go back to the Scriptures and see what they say and to talk much more about why we think what we do. Sometimes, we recognise there are skills and experiences within the church membership that would be helpful, particularly where we have none ourselves relating to the matter at hand. Sometimes seeking the advice of the deacons will help. One way or the other, we have always come to an agreed position in the end. The issue is not disagreement – which is inevitable – but the manner in which you disagree and the means you find to resolve it.

But disagreement is not just inevitable, it is healthy. It is a very worrying sign indeed if an eldership never disagrees on anything. This can only be the product of a handful of possible causes, none of which are good. It may well speak to a domineering 'lead elder' that everybody is too afraid to disagree with. It may speak to a lack of vision that means nobody ever proposes anything new and therefore there is never anything to disagree over. It may speak to an unwillingness on the part of the elders to take any responsibility for anything and so they happily cede every matter to whoever proposes it. Obviously, disagreement for disagreement's sake is no good. Nor is having a belligerent attitude that automatically opposes matters come what may. But, in general, disagreement is healthy. It shows an investment in the ministry from your elders: they care enough to say when something isn't right. It shows a desire to seek to do what is right, rather than just whatever is proposed. It shows that nobody is so dominant as to never be challenged. It shows a willingness to accept responsibility and stand by decisions. It shows people are coming up with new ideas that warrant critique. Ultimately, though it may seem to make life harder much of the time, disagreement on an eldership is healthy.

Chapter 16:

The Relationship of Elders with Deacons

Before we look at the relationship between elders and deacons, we need to look at what a deacon is and what they are there to do. The word translated deacon (Greek: *diakonos*) doesn't help us much because it just means *servant*. It was commonly used to denote a servant of a king, making it an appropriate term for people in the church serving King Jesus. As we look at how the Bible uses the word in the church context, all manner of people doing all sorts of things are called deacons. Of the 29 times the word is used in the New Testament, at least 25 of them do not refer to any particular position in the church. However, what is clear from 1 Timothy 3 – following the qualifications for elders – is that some in the church are to be set aside for diaconal work. Just as for elders, there are qualifications for their appointment that set them apart from the rest of the church. Much as we might like to consider everyone a deacon because every member is a servant of the church, clearly there is a distinct diaconal role outlined in 1 Timothy 3.

Many consider Acts 6:1–7 to be the appointment of the first deacons. Some call these seven men proto-deacons. Others are hesitant to refer to the seven that way because the Greek noun *diakonos* is not used. However, the verb *diakoneō* (to serve) is applied to what these seven men do (Acts 6:2). Just as the word marriage is not used anywhere in the early chapters of Genesis, but everybody recognises Adam and Eve were certainly married, so the word deacon is not used in Acts 6:1–7 but what these men do, and the words used to describe what they are doing, suggest they are deacons. As there were no elders in the Jerusalem church at this point, some argue the seven could not be deacons. But the Apostles themselves were acting as overseers at this point, later establishing elders who would lead the church after them. What we see in Acts 15, for example, is part of the Apostles handing authority in the church over to the elders. That is why James has the final word and not Peter. Furthermore, Acts 6:1–7 seems to have provided a pattern that was continued in the early church.

It is clear from Acts 6:1–2, where a dispute arose over the distribution of food to the needy, that the primary role of the Apostles was a focus on preaching the word. The issue was not that serving tables was beneath the Apostles, but it made no sense for them to be taken away from their primary focus on word-ministry. The Apostles' solution was to appoint deacons to manage the food distribution so they could continue to focus on the word. This is significant when we compare the qualifications for elders and deacons in 1 Timothy 3, where the key distinction between them is the ability to teach. Taken together, elders are called to the oversight of the church with a primary focus on word-ministry and, given the Apostles handed authority in the church over to elders, deacons are to support the ministry of the elders as they did for the Apostles in Acts 6. As Benjamin Merkle puts it, 'it seems best to view the deacons as servants who do whatever is necessary to allow the elders to accomplish their God-given calling of shepherding and teaching the church.'[1]

So, how should elders and deacons relate to one another? In no particular order, here are some things to consider.

Subordinate support

John Benton says:

> The elders of the church are responsible before God for the whole flock in every single department (Acts 20:28). There is no area of which the elders can ultimately say 'that is not our responsibility, it is solely a matter for the deacons'. This is explicit in 1 Timothy 5:17 where without reference to deacons and without qualification, Paul speaks of the elders as 'directing the affairs of the church'.[2]

The role of deacon is subordinate to that of the elders. Deacons exist to support the work of the elders. They are necessarily directed by the elders. They are not free agents to do whatever they will, but exist to help enact the oversight of the eldership and to relieve them of matters that would otherwise take them away from their

1 Merkle, 40 *Questions*, p.240

2 As quoted in Pond, *Only Servants*, p.105

primary responsibilities. However, the elders remain responsible for what the deacons do. The elders may well delegate the running of a ministry or an area of responsibility to the deacons, but it nevertheless remains the case that the elders are still ultimately responsible for what happens within the church.

Distinct and yet close

Given that deacons exist to support the elders, there must be a closeness of relationship. Some churches operate with a board of elders and a committee of deacons and never the twain shall meet. In some instances, diaconal committees act as a brake on the work of elders, functioning like the UK House of Lords through which all business must flow.[3] Whilst the Bible clearly recognises elders and deacons as two separate functions in the church, they are not entirely separate but instead work in tandem. Deacons do not exist to act as an accountability check on the eldership – that authority lies with the church members as a whole – but rather to support and enact the ministry driven by the elders in such a way that the elders are not taken away from word-ministry and pastoral oversight.

If the elders have ultimate responsibility for all that happens within the church, but they may nevertheless delegate responsibilities to the deacons, there necessarily needs to be a

3 For readers outside of the UK: according to the UK Parliament website, 'the House of Lords is the second chamber of UK Parliament. It plays a crucial role in examining bills, questioning government action and investigating public policy.' There is no room biblically for deacons to fulfil a similar role in the life of the church.

close relationship between them. Elders should not micromanage deacons but nevertheless need to be aware of what they are doing. Elders need to extend a level of trust to their deacons. So, elders must work closely with deacons, directing them in how they can support the ministry of the elders, while avoiding micromanaging those who are called to relieve them of responsibility, which would undermine the point of having deacons altogether.

General, not specific

As we have seen, the role of deacons is a general one. They exist to do whatever is required to help the elders shepherd and teach the church. It is overly simplistic to limit diaconal work to 'practical' matters. Indeed, Acts seems to present the proto-deacons – men such as Philip and Stephen – as having particularly powerful evangelistic word-ministries. Deacons are not merely limited to undertaking practical and administrative work but are to serve generally in ways that would free the elders to fulfil their specific calling.

This means there may be times in which deacons are drawn into spiritual and pastoral work. Sometimes, the elders may feel the deacons have particular insight into a matter that would help them determine what to do and so they seek their input. There may be pastoral issues that the deacons are well placed to handle. Perhaps one particular deacon is especially close to the person involved or maybe one of the deacons has a particular temperament or disposition that is lacking on the eldership and they would therefore be a helpful supporting person in addressing a specific pastoral matter. The point here is that deacons are not mere dogsbodies.

They may take on significant administrative and practical duties in order to free the elders up to focus on their primary calling. But they may also take on various spiritual matters in the church under the direction of the elders for the purpose of supporting them in their ministry too. Whatever would serve the elders, under their direction, the deacons may get involved.

United but separate

If elders are to meaningfully delegate responsibilities to deacons, there must be opportunity for deacons to actually get on with what they have been given to do. More to the point, if elders are to actually be freed up to fulfil their calling, it will not help to have the deacons continually calling and asking what the elders would do – that would mean the elders may as well have done the thing themselves! At the same time, if deacons are to work under the direction of the elders without becoming a separate entity, some means of unifying the work of the elders and deacons must exist.

There are all sorts of ways to achieve this. In my own church, the elders meet weekly and ensure that we are keeping a handle on the various matters affecting the church and its members. Though expected to have a general willingness to handle any perceived gaps in ministry, each deacon has a specific area of ministry delegated to them by the elders. Though the deacons are expected to simply get on with their particular areas of ministry, the elders and deacons meet together every quarter to make sure the work of ministry is progressing. This allows freedom for the deacons to get on with the work they have been given without unnecessary interference whilst maintaining the vital link between elders and deacons. Further to this, there is a general 'open door' policy where any of the deacons may come to the elders and raise any matter that might need addressing in the church.

I don't present any of this as the only right or exclusively biblical way. It is merely one way. Readers may find that other setups work better in their context. The point is, however you achieve it, make sure there is enough freedom for deacons to get on with their work so the elders are actually freed up to fulfil their calling whilst maintaining a link with the deacons to avoid working in silos and at cross-purposes.

Chapter 17:

The Relationship of Elders with Women

We have not yet addressed the biblical demand for elders to be men (not women) which stems from a complementarian understanding of Scripture. The word complementarianism doesn't appear anywhere in the Bible in the same way the word trinity cannot be found. However, it is a summary term for the biblical teaching that God has made men and women equal in value but different in function. That is, they are both important and complement one another. The most obvious and least controversial example of this concerns having children. It requires both a man and a woman to make a child. Neither one is more important than the other, but neither can do what only the other is able. God made men and women complementary to fulfil different, yet equally important, functions.

More controversially - but nevertheless biblically - complementarianism says that there is a distinction to be made between men and women in both the church and the home. There is much we could say about what that does and doesn't mean in practice, none of which is pertinent to our discussion here. What is relevant is that Scripture calls men alone to the role of eldership in the local church. Specifically, 1 Timothy 2:12 says, 'I do not allow a woman to teach or to have authority over a man'. Given the fundamental word-ministry and authority that comes with being an elder, a straightforward reading excludes women from this ministry function of church life. Nor can we dismiss this as a mere cultural concern because Paul roots his instruction in the created order not in cultural issues or particular problems in the church to which he is writing (cf. 2:13–14). It is also hard to escape the continual use of masculine pronouns running throughout the eldership qualifications in 1 Timothy 3:1–7 and Titus 1:6–9 which point to male-only eldership. If it is merely a local, cultural matter for the church in Ephesus where Timothy is based, it begs the question why these same instructions are given to Titus five hundred miles away in Crete. A plain reading of Scripture is that eldership is to be male only.

Much more could, of course, be said about this – there are books exclusively devoted to this issue. The reason I raise it is not to defend the position here but because biblical complementarianism raises legitimate practical questions. If elderships are male-only, how can they meaningfully relate to women in the church? The question is even more pressing in certain communities. Working-class British culture is much more matriarchal than middle-class British culture. How are all-male elderships supposed to connect with anyone in those female-dominant communities? What is an all-male eldership supposed to do when single mothers come into the church and there is no husband with whom a male-only eldership can relate to the family? The same issues arise when it comes to engaging with Muslim women and others from cultures where cross-gender relationships are deemed inappropriate. The answer cannot lie in abandoning what Scripture demands, but the questions for the church and wider community must be faced because they have real world implications.

Many churches, recognising these issues, have been moved to employ women's workers. If not formally employing one, they may nevertheless have a *de facto* women's worker who functionally takes on the role. Sometimes this is the pastor's wife, though there is no biblical reason why it must be (more on which in the next chapter). Other times, this is somebody recognised by the church as particularly suitable for the task. A women's worker can provide a helpful first point of contact for women in the church and may well deal with many pastoral issues. The elders may be informed or brought into discussions where appropriate by the women's worker.

This is, of course, all well and good. But it doesn't change the fact that a women's worker – though without question a helpful and legitimate role – is not a strictly biblical function. That doesn't make the role wrong or valueless. Most of us have no problem with a church secretary or administrator, neither of which are mentioned in Scripture either and both of which exist for entirely pragmatic reasons. Some (depending on their understanding of the diaconal qualifications) are happy to make a women's worker part of the diaconate. Whilst this puts the women's worker into an explicitly biblical role, it still doesn't take us away from the fact – as we saw in the previous chapter – that deacons serve under the authority of the elders. As such, the elders still need proper oversight of a women's worker and to have some understanding of the issues going on in the church for them to have biblical oversight of the membership at large. Consequently, if you have a women's worker (whether formally or informally), you need some system that allows feedback and regular review between the worker and the elders. It would not be helpful or good to have a ministry that operates entirely out of view of the elders, with a pastoral function that the elders have no real knowledge about or involvement in. This doesn't mean everything must be relayed to the elders – a good women's worker will have the sense to know when a matter needs to be discussed with the eldership and when it doesn't – but there must be a way for appropriate matters to be considered by the eldership where required.

But what if the church cannot employ a women's worker and there is nobody suitable, or in a position, to take on this role in the church? An all-male eldership still needs to relate to its female members. They still have a duty of oversight concerning the souls of women in the church. Female members still need pastoral input. How are all-male elderships to relate to women then?

First, though we often overlook it, we must remember that the primary means of pastoral input are the same for everybody. The weekly gathering of God's people is the first port of call for pastoral input. The preaching of the word is designed not merely to explain a passage of Scripture, but also to apply it to God's people and to cause them to change. Elders – particularly those who take on the primary responsibility for preaching and teaching – must take care to ensure that their sermons are duly applied to the different situations facing men and women in the church. Of course, what happens on a Sunday is more than just preaching. There are other elements of a church meeting all of which are designed to do something in God's people. Again, care should be taken to pick songs and encourage prayers that speak to the various needs and pastoral concerns of the whole congregation.

Outside of a Sunday, there are often other opportunities for pastoral input that are available to all. Many churches have midweek home groups or whole church Bible studies. Just as with the teaching on a Sunday, these occasions ought to allow both men and women to ask questions, engage with the teaching of the church and have the word applied directly to them. My own church also runs a Theology Breakfast, an hour's doctrinal Bible study before the service every Sunday. This is another opportunity for members of the church to come, learn and engage with Scripture. Here they can have questions answered and real issues dealt with. But we should remember that the primary means of pastoral input is the same for all members of the church. Men and women alike can tap into these things. Elders must take care to ensure the teaching they provide does really speak into the issues facing all within the congregation.

Second, clearly there will be issues that cannot be addressed in a sermon or through the usual teaching of the church. There may be matters that arise outside of those meetings. A female member of the church, reasonably and understandably, may want some input from the church elders on a given matter. This sort of help and access must be available to the women of the church as much as it is for the men.

Of course, there are practical concerns to be considered. Some find the 'Billy Graham rule'[1] to be helpful. That is, for a man never to be alone with a woman, particularly in pastoral situations that could lead to bonds forming. Nevertheless, this approach fails to take account of the fact that such things could equally be at issue for a same-sex attracted member of your church. Nor does it account for the fact that – long before any sexually charged inappropriateness may take place – there is a whole raft of potential sin that is much more likely to happen that warrants consideration. Far more pastoral meetings have been marred by anger, emotional manipulation and a range of other sinful behaviours than sexual advances and inappropriate relationships. That is not to say we should be naïve or blind to the possibility of sexual sin – clearly such things do happen – but it is to say that other matters of sin can be more prevalent and just as likely to cause pastoral problems. More to the point, all of these same issues exist for meetings in male-only pastoral settings too. This leads me to conclude that the 'Billy Graham rule' is totally inadequate.

As a general rule, it seems prudent to always have another person in the room for pastoral meetings. This applies whether you are in a male-only setting or you are dealing with a female member. In many countries, including the UK, it is now common practice for doctors to have a system of chaperones to ensure that medical examinations only do what is strictly necessary and are carried out in an appropriate way. They provide this for both men

---

1 Cf. 'What's the Billy Graham Rule?', *The Billy Graham Foundation*, 23rd July 2019, accessed at https://billygraham.org/story/the-modesto-manifesto-a-declaration-of-biblical-integrity/, accessed 04/09/2025

and women. It strikes me there is wisdom here for pastoral matters in the church as well. This is not a women-only issue, but prudent for any pastoral meeting you may have.

In our church, when we conduct interviews for membership, we always have two elders present. We think it is sensible for at least two people to agree to recommend an application. When it comes to pastoral matters, in order to ensure everything is appropriate, we think it is sensible to have two people present. It doesn't always need to be two elders but could be an elder and a suitable trusted woman from the church (whether the elder's wife or someone else) so that pastoral matters are seen and felt to be entirely above board. This approach is a safeguard for elders themselves as well as for the people to whom they are giving counsel. In recent years, elders have been frequently accused of spiritual abuse. Having others in the room with you as you offer pastoral counsel protects elders against unfair accusations when they are simply disagreeing with somebody or not affirming an individual in an opinion or behaviour. Likewise, having other people in the room stops abusive elders from acting inappropriately towards members of the church without repercussions. It may not stop abuse occurring in the first instance, but it should bring the matter into the open. There will be witnesses as to whether what they said and did was inappropriate and this should act as a brake on any inclination towards ungodly behaviour on the part of an elder.

I do not think these things are only an issue when it comes to elders meeting with women. They can apply equally to elders meeting with men in the church too. If you have a women's worker, though they will likely be the first point of contact for women, there will inevitably be times when elders may need to meet with women in the church directly. If you don't have a women's worker, you certainly need to find ways to engage with women in the church. As a general rule of thumb, it seems prudent to always meet – regardless of gender – with others. Should you ever need to meet one-to-one, do this somewhere public like at a cafe. The only unique thing about meeting with women in the church is that it may often be wise to take another woman with you for the meeting. They will have insights and understanding that you may not.

In terms of women's ministry in the church, just as with men, the roles and functions women can fulfil in the church will be dictated primarily by the gifts God has given to them. The same Spirit who empowers men, also empowers women. The same gifts available through the Spirit are also available to women. This means the same acts of service open to men, in essence, will be available to women. They may exercise those gifts in different ways and places within the life of the church, but churches need to be alive to the multitude of ways in which women can and should serve.

Scripture is clear about the roles of men and women in the local church, specifically eldership being restricted to qualified men. Nevertheless, it is worth pointing out that most men will not be church elders. Furthermore, though having women teaching in certain settings would not be appropriate, that does not mean women with teaching gifts cannot exercise them. Titus 2:3–4 specifically speaks about older women teaching younger women and it is evident that Priscilla was involved with her husband Aquila in explaining the way of the Lord more clearly to Apollos on the mission field (cf. Acts 18:24–28). What this means is that women can exercise teaching gifts in appropriate forums. This could be through regular women's discipleship, teaching children or meeting with women in the community. Women are able to teach in the local church, but that teaching should be exercised in appropriate places to appropriate people. Elders should be looking to utilise women's gifts in the church to the fullest possible extent. It cannot be the case that this is always and only ever limited to making church lunches and playing piano. We shouldn't be surprised if women take their gifts and find fulfilment in other places to the detriment of the local church when they are unnecessarily limited beyond any restriction of Scripture.

It is good and right to look at how all members' gifts can be utilised within the church but secular work is also God's provision for the local church. Every church needs people within it who are working in secular jobs in order to support the financial needs of the church and to be good witnesses in those places. At times, one member of a family may earn more so that another is freed up for the work of ministry. In time past, it was usually the husband who earned and the wife who was freed up to serve in various ways in the church. However, that is often not the case today. As Clifford Pond says, 'When roles are reversed in the home, the wife being the money earner, the husband may be released for work in the church for which he is suited. All this may be seen as part of the loving providence of God.'[2] Interestingly, this was (for a time) my own situation. Prior to being called by Oldham Bethel Church to be their pastor, my wife was the chief earner in our home. That setup freed me to do more work in the church than I otherwise would

2 Pond, *Only Servants*, p.113

have been able. This freedom to serve and utilise my gifts within the church was a significant part in my becoming a pastor. Had God, in his sovereignty, not made my wife the chief earner in our home for that time, it is unlikely I would be in ministry now. There are such examples in the New Testament, like Lydia, who ran her own business and apparently supported the local church through it.

Nevertheless, in the New Testament we see women being given meaningful roles and functions within the church. Phoebe is described as 'a servant of the church' (Rom. 16:1). Some take the Greek word translated servant (Gk. *diakonos*) to mean she was a deacon in the local church and understand 1 Timothy 3:11 to refer to women (Gk. *gunē*)[3] who were also deacons in the church. Even if we do not understand 1 Timothy 3:11 in that way and reckon Phoebe not to be a deacon in the technical sense but a servant of the church more generally, it is clear she had a significant and meaningful role. She is also described by Paul as a 'benefactor of many' (cf. Rom. 16:1–2). The implication here is that she has a meaningful role in the church and is also a woman of means who actively supports ministry financially. Both of these things should be encouraged among women today. They should be encouraged to exercise their gifts to the fullest extent within the church. If they are working women, we should be grateful for them as they are putting themselves in a position to financially support the work of ministry. Working wives should similarly be well regarded for working in order to free their husbands up to serve in the church in ways they might not otherwise be able. Rather than centring on what

3 The Greek word for women and wives, *gunē*, is the same.

women cannot do (which, in all honesty, is not a long or significant list and is actually identical to the majority of men in our churches) we should be looking at the plethora of ways we can encourage women to serve, fully utilising their gifts, and encouraging them in their work both inside and outside of the church.

Chapter 18:

The Relationship of Elders with their Wives

In the previous chapter, we highlighted complementarianism and how this has an impact on the relationships between elders and female members of the church. But this doctrine also has an impact on elders and how they relate to their wives. In turn, how elders relate to their wives has an impact on how they relate to the church and how the church relates to the elder and his wife. We will look at how elders and their wives relate to one other in three different areas: interpersonally, contextually and publicly.

Interpersonally

When I speak about the interpersonal angle of how elders relate to their wives, I am principally speaking about what the Bible says to elders about this issue. That is, what does the Bible say about how elders and their wives are to love and relate to one another interpersonally within their marriage?

The Bible states that husbands are head of their wives. A lot can be said about this, but in essence husbands are called to love their wives as Christ loved the church whilst wives are to submit to their husbands in the context of that love (Eph. 5:22–23). The submission of the wife to her husband is not some servile, second-class citizenship in the home. Rather, Jesus' sacrificial love for his church is the model. This means, in the ordinary run of things, a husband is to lay down his life for his wife. He is to love her as Christ loved the church. He is to set aside his own wants, needs and desires and lead in such a way that allows his wife to willingly submit to his leadership because it is a loving, sacrificial leadership that causes his spouse to flourish. That's the kind of leadership – wherever it's coming from – most of us would gladly submit ourselves to. Indeed, there is mutual submission involved as the husband who loves his wife that well will submit to her needs and desires much of the time. It bears saying, he can only know what these things are and then submit to them if his wife is meaningfully involved in their decision-making.[1]

Most significantly for our discussion, managing one's household well is an important qualification for eldership. God holds husbands and fathers uniquely responsible for the spiritual state of their houses and will hold them accountable for how they led their wives and children. Whilst leadership can be authoritarian, it can also be consensual. Similarly, leadership can be about making decisions

1 Much of this material I wrote some time ago for my blog. Kneale, S., 'Complementarianism and answering Beth Moore's valid questions', *Building Jerusalem*, 22nd July 2020 accessed at https://buildingjerusalem.blog/2020/07/22/complementarianism-and-answering-beth-moores-valid-questions/, accessed 04/09/2025

or it can involve delegation (which, of course, is a decision of itself). Good leadership – or, more specifically good household management (a qualification necessary to be an elder) – is far more than just making good decisions and insisting everyone else carry out our orders. In my view, if your wife is an accountant and maths is not a strong point for you, it is good household management to delegate the role of looking after your cash to your wife and decidedly bad leadership to insist on a gendered view of activities that the Bible doesn't, such that you undertake that role and mess up your finances.[2]

Therefore, we can say that the Lord holds husbands and fathers ultimately accountable for how their home is managed. But he will hold them accountable for the decisions they take – whether they insisted on doing everything or they delegated things to their spouses – and he will hold them responsible for whether they utilised their spouse's God-given gifts for the good of their family and to God's glory or not. He will hold them accountable for whether they were making decisions and doing things because they are arrogant or whether they were delegating responsibilities because they are feckless and lazy. In the end, he calls husbands and fathers to lead their families so they flourish, so they can best

---

2 This material is largely taken from my blog. I recommend reading the posts referenced in footnotes 1 & 2 in full to see how I understand complementarianism works out in practice in the home. Kneale, S., 'Is this approach to complementarianism just dressed up egalitarianism?', *Building Jerusalem*, 13th May 2022 accessed at https://buildingjerusalem.blog/2022/05/13/is-this-approach-to-complementarianism-just-dressed-up-egalitarianism/, accessed 11/09/2025

glorify God through the gifts and personalities he has given them, and to manage their households well (which necessarily includes all those things).

I do not think it is failing to take headship seriously, nor acting like an egalitarian, to let those who are better placed or qualified to decide certain matters do so. That is good leadership, good household management. The Lord will still hold husbands accountable. He will hold them to account for how well their families flourish. He will hold them to account for how well they shepherded their families to glorify God with their gifts. He will hold them to account for the arrogance or laziness of their decision-making and their reasons for taking upon themselves, or giving away, responsibilities. When we realise this, the specific jobs done or the person whose voice ought to be most clearly heeded in any given situation is not really the point at issue. The issue is how well the head, whom the Lord holds accountable, managed those things for the good of his family.

Paul is explicit in 1 Timothy 3:5 about the reason why good household management is an eldership criterion. He says, 'If anyone does not know how to manage his own household, how will he take care of God's church?' In other words, how it goes in the home is how it will go in the church. If a man is an abusive and domineering husband, it's likely he will be an abusive and domineering elder. If a man is an authoritarian in the home who demands to make every decision, he's likely to be an authoritarian church leader who seeks to make every decision. If a husband infantilises his wife, just imagine what he will do to a church that is supposed to grow up to maturity in Christ. If a man refuses to allow his wife to fully utilise her gifts for God's glory, what approach will he take towards members of the church using their gifts for God's glory? This is why, though the Lord restricts eldership to men, a proper understanding of complementarianism matters, because our approach to headship with our wives will necessarily be an indicator of what we will be like in the church. Elders are called to love their wives like Christ loved the church, to serve their spouse's needs ahead of their own, to help them flourish, grow up to maturity in Christ and glorify God through the exercise of the gifts they have been given. These are the very same things elders are called to do in the church.

Contextually

When it comes to elders and their wives, it should be stressed that context and circumstance will play a big role in determining exactly what any couple might do to navigate the issues that come with serving on an eldership. I am extremely wary of laying down red lines and rules that the Bible doesn't. I am convinced Scripture is careful not to say too much on the specifics of these things because they will necessarily work out differently across cultures, contexts and according to a variety of circumstances. Nevertheless, let me land on a few common things and try to apply these biblical principles of headship to those situations.

Inevitably, there will be some tension between the demands of eldership and the needs of our family. Just as in secular employment, sometimes the wishes and desires of your family cannot be met because of your work. The same is true for the church. There will be times you cannot do certain things with your family because of the demands of ministry. However, in the same way as many men abandon their familial responsibilities in favour of their work, stories abound of pastors' families who have grown to hate the church because the pastor only ever seemed to have time for ministry and never for them. It is not at all uncommon to hear of families being sacrificed on the altar of ministry; wives and children left behind in the wake of all-encompassing church work. Let me be frank, this is neither right nor godly. Jesus does not ask elders to forsake their families for the sake of the church. In fact, he demands the very opposite. You are only qualified to be an elder in the church if you are functioning as a good husband and father. If your wife and children feel neglected, if you are not caring for your family as you ought because you pour all your energy into church life and ministry, you have disqualified yourself – at least for a time – from leadership in the local church. As has often been said, your church can get another elder but your wife and children cannot get another husband or father.

Even taking the caveats above into account, pastors' wives do inevitably have a unique role in the church. In Genesis 2:18 we read, 'Then the Lord God said, "It is not good for the man to be alone. I will make a helper corresponding to him."' All wives are called to be a help to their husbands and this corresponds to all aspects of life.[3] What makes a pastor's wife unique is simply that she is married to the pastor of the church. She is, therefore, uniquely placed to be a

3 NB: we need to be careful not to react wrongly to the word 'helper'. In biblical usage, it doesn't denigrate or suggest inferiority. There is no implication of 'help' meaning 'busy work' that we might give a child thus implying the infantilisation of women. The word 'helper' is most commonly used of God and his role in serving his people. Wives are called to be their husband's helper just as God is his people's helper.

help to the pastor. In essence, she is to support her husband and help him in his work of ministry so far as possible. There are lots of ways pastors' wives can be helpful and supportive although these things will depend on their particular situation, context and gifting. As mentioned above, being willing to take on extra childcare to free their husband to do the work of eldership is a significant help if you have children. Working to bring in extra money as one is able – like the Proverbs 31 wife of noble character – can be helpful to a pastor's ministry because it takes away concerns about finances and allows him to focus on the work of ministry. Providing encouragement and critical feedback on sermons should be welcomed, especially getting a woman's insight on sermon application. It is helpful for pastors' wives to give insight on pastoral meetings with other women, helping her husband address issues with women in the church in the best way. Similarly, they can offer a woman's perspective on matters of church life more broadly. Whilst they won't speak for all women, there will inevitably be things that men will not notice or consider important that might be significant for the women in the church. Having someone highlight these things is genuinely helpful and should be well received. Wherever she may be helpful, a pastor's wife will serve her husband and her church well by doing those things as she is able.

Another key way in which a pastor's wife can help and support her husband is to act as a sounding board more generally. Some believe that elders' business is so secret that it should not even be shared with their wives. I agree fully with Clifford Pond when he says, 'I believe there are very few items, if any, that elders should not discuss privately with their wives. If an elder has not sufficient discretion to know when absolute secrecy has to be observed, I doubt if he should be an elder. If an elder's wife has not the ability to keep quiet about matters shared with her by her husband, again, I doubt if her husband should be an elder.'[4] If an elder is called to self-control, blamelessness and good sense, that must include knowing when a matter must be kept absolutely secret or can be shared with his wife. Similarly, if he is called to good household management, that must include not only knowing when it is appropriate to share a matter with his wife but knowing her ability to keep private matters to herself. If his wife is unable to be discreet, and yet he continues to share matters with her, he appears not to be qualified based on these eldership criteria. Few churches – quite rightly – would appoint a man to eldership whose wife was an indiscreet gossip because of the evident problems that would cause in the church. It wouldn't help his ministry, it would not encourage anyone to share anything sensitive, nor would it engender confidence in his leadership. Assuming an elder does meet these qualifications means there is no reason why he should not be able to share matters with his wife, as long as this does not place undue burdens on her or their marriage. Let me lay out a few broad principles to help us think that last little but significant caveat through.

It bears saying your wife has not been called as an elder of the church; you have! That fact alone should temper what we might choose to share. If you debrief your wife after every elders' meeting, run every decision that is ever taken past her for approval, you are in effect treating your wife as a *de facto* elder. That is neither whom

4 Pond. *Only Servants*, p.112

the church has called nor helpful to your wife. She doesn't, in fact, have the ability to implement her views in the way you do because she is not an elder. To load her with all the burdens of eldership, without the same ability to do anything about them, is neither fair nor right.

However, if an issue is seriously affecting you mentally or emotionally, your wife almost certainly needs to know about it. If you're struggling, your wife needs to know at a minimum that it isn't her fault and it is a heavy church matter that is weighing on you. There are all manner of things your wife probably doesn't need to know and certainly doesn't have to know, but if it is causing a change in your demeanour or behaviour and is clearly causing you distress, particularly if it has potential to impact your relationship, it is almost certainly something she needs to know both for the sake of your marriage and so she can best help you as you seek to deal with the matter.

Things that you can carry emotionally without it having any great effect on you do not necessarily need to be shared with your wife. That isn't to say you can't speak about such things with her, just that she doesn't need to be burdened with them and, if they are liable to be a burden to her, why share it when there is no need to do so? Likewise, you don't want to share anything unnecessary that will impact your wife's ability to love the church and serve with joy. If an issue is not a matter of great mental or emotional stress to you, but it has potential to negatively impact your wife's ability to love people and serve joyfully, what good will come of sharing that kind of thing?

I don't want to say any more here. I recognise the specifics of what any elder might share with his wife will be tempered by a whole variety of personal and contextual factors. The Bible avoids setting arbitrary rules on this and it is certainly above my paygrade to create any! Rather, I want to offer some broad yet prudential practical principles to help us balance the biblical teaching on eldership and headship whilst respecting the role of wives who are called to be helpers in a shared ministry with their husband.[5] I trust you will be able to apply these things to your situation appropriately as issues – such as personal criticism or heavy church matters – inevitably rear their head in your context.

It is worth a brief word on the broader issue of confidentiality at this point. This issue extends beyond what an elder might share with his wife. There is often an assumption of complete and strict confidentiality in anything shared with an elder. I suspect this owes something to the (unbiblical) Catholic teaching on confession. Confidentiality in the confessional is taken so seriously by the Catholic Church that some of its priests have been defrocked for reporting criminal offences that have been confessed to them. As Protestant churches believe in the priesthood of all believers, and recognise Jesus to be the only mediator between God and man (cf. 1 Tim. 2:5), sin is to be confessed directly to him. There is, therefore, no obligation to confess to any other priest, nor any need for the seal of the confessional, because sins are not confessed to or through your elders. However, given what we have said about gossip above, it is reasonable to expect discretion from your elder

---

5 Refer back to footnote 3.

nor would many people seek his counsel if it became apparent he had no seal on his mouth.

The truth is, it is rarely if ever a good idea for elders to promise complete confidentiality. Our job is to serve people and not harm them. We are called to steward the information people share with us for their good. That necessarily means there will be times we will not pass on information because it would harm the person who shared it with us, but there will also be times we will pass on the information because failing to do so would lead to harm. So, when it comes to pastoral counsel, we must essentially ask our members to trust us to serve their good and seek to do all we can to avoid any harm. For this reason, an indiscreet elder is not qualified for the role because he is using information in a way that harms the members entrusted to his care. An elder with an indiscreet wife, or an elder who hasn't the sense to know when he can and can't share a matter with her, is similarly going to end up harming his people with the information they share with him, which also disqualifies him.

Whilst we have focused here on what an elder might share with his wife, what a wife might share with her husband is important too. It is inevitable that some will share matters with elders' wives. This can bring a whole host of issues with it. Some will (wrongly) believe that if they tell an elders' wife something then it has necessarily been passed on to the elder. Church members wanting to speak to their elders about an issue should speak to them directly. It is unfair to expect his wife to pass on your news and, not to put too fine a point on it, this can often be a cowardly way to avoid more awkward conversations. There is nothing wrong with sharing whatever you want with an elders' wife, but if it is a matter for the elders you should go to them directly. Nevertheless, there may be things shared with an elder's wife that are not deemed for the elders by the person sharing. This can put elders' wives in an awkward position if it is something *she feels* the elders need to know. In these kinds of situations, the comments on confidentiality above apply similarly to elders' wives and the same factors that influence an elder's decision to share a matter with his wife will most likely be relevant when the shoe is on the other foot. However, this kind of situation highlights some of the unique pressures that may be at play in ministry families. Elders' wives – just as much as elders – need someone they can share with too. Just as an elder might share with his wife when these kind of pressures are becoming difficult so his wife – if she is being confided in and this is causing her anxiety – should be able to openly share with her husband. In so doing, they may sympathise with one another and seek to build in healthy pressure-release strategies for their own marriage and wider ministry.

Publicly

So far, we have been thinking about how elders and their wives relate to one another in the home and how they might operate behind closed doors in the different church contexts in which they find themselves. However, we also need to think about how elders and their wives relate to one another in the public-facing aspects of ministry. Here, we are not thinking about how they speak and relate to one another at home so much as how elders and their wives can serve one another when it comes to the public aspects of ministry life as well as how church members view the public-facing aspects of an elder's family life.

It is almost inevitable that ministry demands will mean an elder is required at many meetings and their wives may be left home alone to deal with any children. As Clifford Pond says:

> If the husband is a leader in the church and as a consequence is frequently absent from the family, he must be very sensitive to the burden this places on his wife. There must be mutual support and encouragement and each must be willing to sacrifice the other's company for the Lord's sake and his church, but none of this should be taken for granted or allowed to go on unchecked.[6]

Every effort should be made to mitigate this where possible. If a man can help deal with the children before going out to the meeting so that this is not all on his wife, this would be a helpful way of loving and serving her. Likewise, in teenage years, being emotionally available for the children, as well as perhaps being physically available for some things too e.g. school events or social activities is right and proper. It is vitally important to wisely balance the competing needs of the church with the different seasons of family life. Similarly, it is good – not just for the family but as a model for the church – to see an elder staying home at least some of the time with his children in order to allow his wife to attend the prayer meeting, Bible study or whatever it may be. Whilst

6 Pond, *Only Servants*, p.111

the family will inevitably sacrifice some time together because of ministry, it is also perfectly reasonable for an elder who has been out at meetings most nights of the week to say 'no' to yet another one so that he is able to spend some time with his family. Churches that have no slack on these things must contend with the fact that they are forcing their elders into sin by making them attend so many meetings that they cannot spend adequate time with their families and, as a result, cannot do what Jesus calls all husbands and fathers to do. Elders should be able to raise this if and when it happens, but churches themselves must take some responsibility for punishing workloads that may ruin families and, in some cases, create barriers for children growing to love the local church.

Coupled to this, churches need to be aware that we now live in a two-income economy and, as a result, many pastors' wives continue in secular work. This should not be seen (as some seem to view it) as robbing the church of a two-for-the-price-of-one worker, but rather as part of freeing the minister from financial concerns so that he is able to focus on the work of ministry. It is the hard work of many pastors' wives continuing in the secular workplace that allows churches to employ full-time pastors at all because they make up the shortfall in whatever the church is able to provide financially. Far from taking from the church, this should rightly be viewed as proper service to the church in freeing their pastor from financial concerns so that he can be more effective in the work of ministry. However, Clifford Pond further points out:

> increasingly nowadays both husband and wife are in employment; this may be necessary to bring adequate money into the home or it may be the right use of gifts

> the Lord has given; but where for whatever reason, husband and wife are both working, the demands of leadership in the church can become an even greater stress.[7]

It should be noted there is no biblical office of pastor's wife. A pastor's wife is, therefore, not a ministry function of the church; it is a description that this woman is married to a pastor. The demands and expectations on a pastor's wife, then, should not exceed the demands on other members of the church. As with any member of the church, the first consideration must be the gifts the Lord has given her. A pastor's wife should be able to exercise her gifts as far as possible within the life of the church; just as she uses them to help her family flourish so she should seek to use them to help her church flourish.

Often, churches forget that pastors' wives may also work full-time jobs and this must be understood when it comes to their service in the church. If she is in full-time work for the sake of her family, and to the benefit of the church in freeing her husband from financial concerns, the church must be careful not to put undue pressure on her to serve more than others who are also working. If a pastor's wife is not in full-time work, she should not be expected to serve more than other members of the church who are also not in full-time work. There should be no more expectation on a pastor's wife than there is on other members of the church in similar situations.

---

7 Ibid.

It must also be remembered, in light of the fact a pastor or elder himself may rightly be required at many meetings and events, any extra ministries a pastor's wife picks up is in addition to the ministry of her husband. This will necessarily eat further into their ability to spend time together as a family. That is not to say a pastor's wife should never be asked to do anything, just that churches need to be mindful of this. Every evening and weekend the pastor is required to be out of the home is time away from his family. Any ministry picked up by the pastor's wife represents further time away from the family in addition to the pastor's duties. Churches should not judge what pastors' wives do visibly in the church, but would do well to reckon that every meeting her husband attends, or every evening he is out of the home on church business, is also ministry she is involved in on behalf of the church, by caring for their children and/or sacrificing time with her husband so that he can adequately serve God's people.

There are some simple steps churches can take to help with all this. At the most basic level, simply encouraging your elders' wives by telling them that you recognise the sacrifices they make in family life whenever their husband is not home. Acknowledging overtly that every meeting their husband attends is a night she misses at home with him, and every time she is at a meeting, it is time they miss together too. Similarly, affirm that you see her secular job (if she has one) and are grateful she is able to take a financial burden away from the church. Few UK churches are in a position to pay their pastors a salary comparable to similar professional jobs, so tell your pastor's wife what a blessing she is to the church that she is able to make up what they lack financially.

You can similarly acknowledge and thank her for the particular role she has supporting her husband – whether that is letting him vent to her, her own personal pastoral work with other women in the church that is hard for a male pastor to do, or whatever it may be. These are just some basic acknowledgements that will help pastors' wives feel seen.

You can also help by offering specific support. For example, knowing that pastors and their wives often struggle for time together and are often required at many meetings between them, offer to babysit young children so they are able to enjoy an evening out together. I should stress this does not mean offering to babysit so that the pastor's wife can also come along to meetings with her husband. That is expecting them to rest and relax at work; it is the equivalent of your colleague offering to mind your children so you can work late, and your wife can join you!

Churches can also be supportive by building in flexibility in working patterns. It is not always easy for a pastor to take a regular day off. This could be because of ministry demands such that the pastor ends up working a 7-day week or family circumstances such as elderly parents with significant care needs mean that one day off is not a matter of rest but is spent operating as a carer. There are no end of possible circumstances that might impact and some flexibility from the church is helpful. One simple and supportive measure could be to allow the accrual of days off so that working one necessary 7-day week gives the option of a gentler 5-day week following. Many churches make their pastors office holders to account for this kind of thing, giving them the freedom to organise their hours in such ways that the work gets done but they can have adequate rest. However you accomplish it, actively finding ways to help your elders spend time with their wives, free to speak together and able to relax fully (which usually means without children present) is a good and God-honouring way to encourage healthy relationships between elders and their wives.

In sum, just as with any other member of the church, if a pastor's wife is suitably gifted for a particular role in the church then she should be freed up to do it. She already has a unique role to play in supporting her husband's ministry and these things should not be overlooked by the church as though they were somehow lesser ministries. Neither the church, nor her husband, should pressure her into doing more for the sake of his ministry than would be expected of other members. But where a wife is able to serve, she should be freed up to exercise her gifts accordingly. Where she is working and supporting her husband, not only should the church be mindful not to expect more from her than from other working members, but she should be valued and acknowledged for serving the church in that way by freeing her husband from financial worries to the wider benefit of the church.

Chapter 19:

Personal, Physical and Mental Wellbeing

We have seen that elders have spiritual responsibility and oversight over the members of the church. We have also looked at how they are to operate in different relationships within the church. But a question often raised is this: who pastors the pastor and who cares for the elders? If our church is operating biblically, with a plurality of elders, the answer is the elders serve one another in this way. In the end, the benefit of plural eldership is significantly diminished if the elders do not watch out for one another.

We should be careful not to suggest that pastoral ministry is harder than other jobs. Every job has its stresses and strains and we shouldn't be too quick to claim unique stress for the pastorate. And yet, many people who have been in some quite high-powered and stressful jobs are adamant that full-time church ministry is an altogether different beast. There is something all-encompassing about it and its relational strains are not so easily left at the door once the bell sounds for home time. Whilst that of itself is not unique – other jobs can feel the same – there are some unique things about pastoral ministry that make it particularly prone to inducing certain issues.

Perhaps one of the more obvious problems is that ministers are not very good at caring for themselves. In their concern to care for others, they frequently don't think about their own health. One of the things elderships can do is remind one another that neglecting our own bodies is neither godly nor right. God made us body and soul and we need to show proper care for both if we are going to have a long and fruitful ministry. Three areas that are frequently ignored but which have a serious and detrimental effect on health and ministry are: eating, sleeping and relaxation. These are not the only areas to think about but they are among the most routinely ignored.

There are two potential problems when it comes to eating regular meals in pastoral ministry. On the one hand, sheer busyness can militate against finding time to eat; on the other, countless meetings and visits often come with food of one sort of another. Some, in a bid to offset the problem of constantly eating, become gluttons of delicacy. They end up on faddy diets and become fussy among God's people. Others throw caution to the wind and pay no heed to ever expanding waistlines and guzzle down all that comes their way, caring nothing for whatever health implications might come with this approach. But whether it is over-eating or constantly thinking about how to manage our weight, we can easily end up making a god out of our bellies.

The implications for our ministry should be obvious. If we are fussy about food that we are offered in people's houses, it can make ministry awkward. At the same time, if our stomachs are rumbling and we are getting hangry whilst trying to counsel somebody, this is just as bad. Sticking to regular meals, not over-indulging and avoiding obsessive talk about calorie counting and diets will all help. Very little will undermine your physical health and ability to carry out your pastoral duties so easily as refusing to eat sensibly.

Another area where pastors are often not very disciplined is sleep. It can be hard to unwind when your mind is full of pastoral issues and church matters. It can be tempting to look at all the things that need to be done and burn the candle at both ends. But as Don Carson has said, 'we are whole, complicated beings; our physical existence is tied to our spiritual well-being, to our mental outlook, to our relationships with others, including our relationship with God. Sometimes the godliest thing you can do in the universe is get a good night's sleep—not pray all night, but sleep.'[1] An unhealthy attitude to sleep may speak to a belief that things will fall apart without us or that important matters will not get done. At the end of the day, sleep is God's way of reminding us every day that he can get on with upholding the universe just fine without us.

Lack of sleep most clearly becomes a problem when we cannot function properly. Clearly, not everybody needs the same amount of sleep. But we can tell if we haven't had enough by how functional we are. If we are the kind of person who becomes more irritable when we haven't slept enough, then it is our duty to ensure we get enough sleep. Indeed, it is an act of love towards those we will deal with tomorrow to sleep properly today. Others of us may find we feel sick or cannot concentrate properly when we haven't slept

1 Carson, D.A., *Scandalous: The Cross and Resurrection of Jesus*, Inter-Varsity Press, Nottingham, UK, 2010, p.147

enough. Again, we are called to do our work as to the Lord, which includes sleeping well enough to do so. If our work is becoming slipshod and – despite thinking more hours necessarily equate to more work – we are actually less productive because we are too tired, then it is incumbent on us to get a good night's sleep.

A third area that frequently falls off the radar is rest and relaxation. In his book *Crazy Busy* Kevin DeYoung recounts the following story:

> We came to the end of our weekly meeting, and I could tell that Jason had something uncomfortable to say ... We had gone through the agenda for over an hour when Jason told me he had one more thing he wanted to talk about.
>
> 'Kevin, are you taking your day off?'
>
> I told him what my plan was and how the last couple of weeks were exceptionally hectic and full of surprises. Jason was sympathetic and the furthest thing from legalistic, but he pressed in a little further.
>
> 'You need to take a day off.'
>
> 'I often do.'
>
> 'Every week.'
>
> 'Well, I was taking Mondays off, but now my kids are in school I switched to Saturdays so I can spend the day with them. But sermon prep always spills over into Saturday. I've been trying to spend extra time at home a couple of mornings a week. And my schedule can be flexible to come home during lunch if I need to.'

> 'You need a day off,' my friend said to me one more time. 'Whatever your theology of the Sabbath, you're not being smart. You can't keep this up.'
>
> 'I know. I know. You're right. Something has to change.'[2]

I share the story in full because it is incredibly common to hear pastors recount some version of this. Pastors are notoriously bad at taking proper time off. Most are already expected to work 6 days a week and many simply forget, or refuse, to take their one day a week with any regularity. As the friend who rightly challenged Kevin DeYoung said, it's just not smart and no one can keep it up. One of the kindest things elders can do for one another is to remind each other to take proper rest.

The problem extends beyond a weekly day off. Many pastors struggle to take their full holiday allowances too. Not only is this detrimental to family life, but it is not helpful for ministry. An unrested pastor is an ineffective pastor. Alongside encouraging one another to take proper weekly rest, elders do well to help each other ensure they are taking regular breaks throughout the year too.

Far and away the biggest issue that puts church leaders out of ministry altogether is poor mental health. A piece of research by Lifeway in 2022 said over 1 in 4 pastors had struggled with some sort of mental health issue. This number is almost identical to their

2 DeYoung, K., *Crazy Busy*, Inter-Varsity Press, Nottingham, UK, 2013, pp.89-90

2014 research.[3] Clearly, stress, anxiety and depressive illnesses are prevalent in the pastorate. Clifford Pond notes:

> Elders, especially preaching elders, are always in the public eye and this puts them under pressure. Their family also has the same problem and the elder has the responsibility of caring for his family as well as coping with himself. Then there is the effect of knowing the high expectations people have of their elders both in their conduct and in their ministry. This is especially the case if members have in their minds the example of an outstanding man known to them. A sense of high calling and commitment leads elders to a very full-time occupation ... conscience is a hard taskmaster and elders sometimes allow themselves to feel that an evening at home or a day out with the family is a dereliction of duty.[4]

Beyond these things, eldership can feel lonely. Many pastors and their families feel isolated. Other church members have the freedom to say 'no' to duties in the church, but paid staff members do not usually feel able to do the same. Church leaders can be lightning rods for criticism. Sometimes they receive personal and hurtful comments about the effectiveness of their ministry,

---

3 Pastors have congregational and, for some, personal experience of mental health, LifeWay Research, 2nd August 2022 accessed at https://research.lifeway.com/2022/08/02/pastors-have-congregational-and-for-some-personal-experience-with-mental-illness/, accessed 05/09/2025

4 Pond, *Only Servants*, p.101

their suitability, and decisions they have taken, which can be unwarranted or outright unkind. Some of these things may even spill over into comments about their family. It can feel as though the minister and his family are fair game and nothing can be said in response. It can, at times, feel as though one's livelihood hangs in the balance any time someone takes against you or dislikes the direction the church is taking. All of these things are undoubtedly stressful. People can forget that full-time ministers and their families are just like everyone else: if you cut them – they bleed.

Alongside all these things, there are various other pressures. Many cite financial worries, high expectations and the fact that ministry success is not easily quantifiable (even if it were, it isn't appropriate to judge ministry success by the number of converts or baptisms at any rate!). The temptation to envy others' ministries and compare theirs with ours is ever present. There is the call to higher moral standards, the stakes that go with it and the sense that all eyes are continually watching. All of this can cause real anxiety.

As we have said already, one of the advantages of plural eldership is that other church leaders should be able to empathise and take some of this strain. At a minimum, elders should encourage full-time church leaders to build proper rest into their weekly routines. The guilt of taking time off can be mitigated by other elders not only encouraging rest but actively offering – and showing they are more than happy – to take on what necessarily must drop if the full-time worker is to take a break.

Alongside this, where elders see that another is struggling – or that is the direction in which an elder is heading – being willing to step in and make concrete suggestions is key. Sometimes full-time workers need permission to say 'no' to things, or even to step back for a time. It is important for all the elders to be looking out for each other in this way and giving one another permission to step back where required. Sometimes offering a sabbatical may be in order, so that the full-time worker can have an extended break and recuperate from the stresses of ministry.

Creating a culture of openness on the eldership is also important. Elderships need to be places where each man can share their struggles openly without fear of judgement or a sense that their job will be on the line because of physical or mental imperfection, or dare I say – even because of sin.[5] Elders need to cultivate trust with one another, that they are men who can be relied on rather than feared; and it must be clear that where struggles and strains are raised, help will be forthcoming. Nothing will induce stress and anxiety more than fearing how your elders will react when you are already under strain. None of this, of course, is an excuse for sin. Sin must be addressed and repented of. But we shouldn't expect perfection from our elders, who are – like every other believer – sinners saved by grace.

5 There are, of course, disqualifying sins that should not be ignored. But there are sin issues which are not disqualifying. Elders sin and we should be working to create a culture of openness and support as sinners all in the same boat.

Chapter 20:

Counselling and Discipline

Traditionally, the pastor of the church has been expected to do much, if not all, the visitation in church life. Some point to the seventeenth-century minister Richard Baxter and seek to emulate his model of pastoral visitation and catechesis. He writes, 'We spend Monday and Tuesday, from morning almost to night, in the work, taking about fifteen or sixteen families in a week, that we may go through the parish, in which there are upwards of eight hundred families, in a year.' He goes on to quote the Westminster Assembly of Divines in support of this programme, arguing 'It is the duty of the minister not only to teach the people committed to his charge in public, but privately, and particularly to admonish, exhort, reprove, and comfort them upon all seasonable occasions, so far as his time, strength, and personal safety will permit. He is to admonish them in time of health to prepare for death. And for that purpose, they are often to confer with their minister about the estate of their souls.'[1] This is viewed as the ideal model for the modern church by some.

Personally, I don't think Baxter's model is ideal. It rests upon the minister alone. It is necessarily dependent on the ability and capacity of one man. I believe it is the role of the elders to make disciples, build up the saints and equip them for works of service through the ministry of word and prayer. As the elders seek to equip the saints for works of ministry, members of the church ought to be growing so that they can also engage in the work of making disciples. I am convinced the church will be built to a greater extent when the priesthood of all believers is taken seriously, discipling relationships between church members are the norm and elders are not seen as the unique or primary channels of God's grace in the church. All of which is to say – not that elders should never visit anyone – but that the goal is to disciple members of the church who are able to effectively disciple other members of the church who, in turn, make disciples.

If that is the goal, and we are aiming for members to be able to disciple one another effectively, is there any particular role for visits from elders? I think there is. What Richard Baxter got right is that sermons alone are not enough. Preaching is vitally important, but if the job of an elder is to equip the saints to be disciples who make disciples, Baxter rightly encourages us to see personal work as a vital means of accomplishing this goal.

---

1 Baxter, R, *The Reformed Pastor*, Monergism, p.13 accessed at https://www.monergism.com/thethreshold/sdg/baxter/The%20Reformed%20Pastor%20-%20Richard%20Baxter.pdf, accessed 08/09/2025

In *The Trellis and the Vine*, Colin Marshall and Tony Payne argue against what they call the 'pastor as service-providing clergyman' who is paid to provide professional services, like preaching and private counselling. They note, 'the ministry that takes place in the congregation will be limited to the gifts and capacity of the pastor: how effectively he preaches, and how many people he can personally know and counsel.' They go on to show that this creates a consumerist culture in the church and argue, 'even the good practice of pastoral counselling can become focused on "me" being cared for by the pastor – such that if the assistant minister visits instead, this is not seen as adequate'.[2] It seems to me this is a direct challenge to Richard Baxter's particular approach; he did seem to view this as the preserve of the minister. Nevertheless, what Baxter grasped is that there must be a shift in mindset as to what pastoral visits exist to do.

Payne and Marshall argue that our churches should be 'centres of training where people are trained and taught to be disciples of Christ who, in turn, seek to make other disciples.'[3] They make a case for a model whereby the pastor:

> is not just to provide spiritual services, nor is it his job to do all of the ministry. His task is to teach and train his congregation, by his word and his life, to become disciple-making disciples of Jesus. There is a radical dissolution, in this model, of the clergy-lay distinction. It is not minister and ministered-to, but the pastor and

2 Marshall, C. and Payne, T., *The Trellis and the Vine*, Matthias Media, Sydney, Australia, 2009, p.94-95

3 Ibid, p.99

> his people working in close partnership in all manner of word ministries.'[4]

They maintain 'Pastoral care, in this approach, is also founded on disciples being trained to care for and disciple other Christians.'[5]

If the model advocated in *The Trellis and the Vine* is correct, what is the purpose of pastoral visits? Richard Baxter helpfully pushes us to understand that visitation is for the purpose of equipping the saints for the work of ministry. Baxter's visitation was not centred on counselling, general advice and psychological support. Despite expectations, as previously noted, pastors are not equipped for such things. Rather, pastors and elders are equipped to teach and apply the Scriptures and this is to be their focus. The purpose of visits, then, is to teach and apply the Scriptures to the people they are visiting with the purpose of equipping members to teach and apply the Scriptures to others. The goal in visitation was 'the duty of personal catechizing and instructing the flock.' Baxter said, 'it is but the least part of the Minister's work, which is done in the Pulpit ... To go daily from one house to another, and see how you live, and examine how you profit, and direct you in the duties of your families, and in your preparation for death, is the great work.'[6] In all this, I think he is right. His model may falter on the assumption that this must all be done by the pastor, but his emphasis on personal work is vitally important. Indeed, pastoral visits are primarily for discipleship. They are a means of equipping disciples who disciple

4 Ibid., p.99

5 Ibid., p.100

6 As quoted in Ibid., p.106

and make disciples. If the pastor does this effectively, it should lead to church members visiting church members, helping to equip one another for works of service.

None of this means there is no case for counselling, if by counselling we simply mean applying the word to the lives of the people we are visiting. Baxter was clear that part of the purpose of his visits was instructing and directing his congregation in their duties; that is, what the Bible demands of them. It no doubt involved encouraging people in living for Jesus as well as pointing out sin in their lives and calling them to repentance. These are the ordinary things of church discipline.

Again, if the model we have outlined above is right, church discipline is not the preserve of the elders alone. Though elders may help and guide the church through matters of discipline, particularly formal and serious matters, most church discipline ought to take place from one member to another. This means that elders are not necessarily always involved in matters of church discipline, but they do have a duty to equip their members to navigate their duties as members in matters of discipline.

In my own church's Membership Handbook, church discipline is described in this way:

> There are two aspects to church discipline. First, there is formative discipline. This is the most common form of discipline; it is the process of bringing people to maturity in Christ through positive instruction and teaching (cf. Eph 4:11f). Formative discipline takes place anytime we listen to a sermon (Col 3:16), hear a Bible study, read Scripture (Jam 1:22–25) or engage in Biblical

conversations with church members (Heb 10:24f). This sort of discipline is vital because it helps us to obey the Lord and pursue holiness.

Second, there is corrective discipline. This is the kind of discipline that takes place when somebody sins. It is usually informal, taking place whenever one believer suggests to another that they are straying from God's best. It is typically private and handled discretely. However, in cases where an individual continues in unrepentant sin or engages in public sin that must be dealt with publicly, corrective discipline can become formal and involve the whole church. Examples of this can be found in Matthew 18:15–17, relating to personal sin between members, and 1 Corinthians 5, relating to public sin in the church. Whether corrective discipline is done informally or formally, it is always done to bring a wandering believer back into right relationship with God and his people (cf. Jam 5:19f)

As church members, we all agree to submit to the formative discipline of teaching and instruction as well as the corrective discipline of the wider church membership who have committed to help us honour and obey Jesus in our lives. We recognise that most corrective discipline will take place informally and privately between individual members.[7]

7 Members Handbook, Oldham Bethel Church, first produced 2018, p.19

The handbook has more to say on this, but this section outlines the two distinct kinds of discipline: formative and corrective. More significantly, it highlights that members submit to the corrective discipline of the wider church membership. You will remember from earlier chapters that the right to determine who belongs to the church rests with the church members. So, the primary responsibility for church discipline lies with church members. The role of elders when it comes to church discipline is to equip God's people so that they can fulfil their responsibilities, including those relating to church discipline. This applies equally to both formative and corrective discipline.

There are really only two stages of corrective discipline. First, a person is to be warned and admonished, with suitable time given for them to repent and change. During this stage, the individual should continue in fellowship and receive the privileges of membership. However, if they remain unrepentant, the church should remove such a person from fellowship and they cannot receive the benefits and privileges of membership. This necessarily means they are unable to serve in any ministry of the church and cannot partake of the Lord's Supper.

Let me say briefly, it is in matters of church discipline where open table advocates are most exposed. If we insist that the only scriptural line is to examine oneself, we really have no recourse – even in matters of serious unrepentant sin – to refuse access to the table when an individual examines themself, and in the face of the church saying otherwise, determines they are fine to partake. Close communion, limiting access to the table to those in meaningful church membership, not only guards the table but guards the church in matters of discipline. If we make membership the grounds to partake – that is, the affirmation of the church that here is a believer – we have legitimate grounds to refuse access to the table when an unrepentant individual is sadly removed from membership. Open table advocates break their own principle and, in effect, become partial by judging one non-member acceptable and another unacceptable. Meaningful discipline means properly guarding the table.

If and when a person is removed from membership, they are to be treated like a Gentile (cf. Mt. 18:17) which, to the Jews in Jesus' day was equivalent to treating them like an unbeliever. But the question follows: how are we to treat unbelievers? I think Clifford Pond is right, 'surely with love and with constant prayer and effort towards his or her conversion. There is never a case for harshly writing a person off and refusing any further contact. There is always a case for seeking the restoration of those who have strayed from the Lord and his people.'[8] A person removed from the fellowship should still have access – as we would give to any unbeliever – to services. We still want this person to come under the sound of the gospel. We still want this person to respond to the word. We still want this person to repent. These things will not happen if we simply cut them off and refuse any contact. There is necessarily a change in our relationship with this person. They are no longer in fellowship, they don't have access to the privileges of membership and members ought not to be simply 'hanging out' with them as though nothing has happened. But none of that means they should be cut off from access to the preached word or barred from

8 Pond, *Only Servants*, p.121

meeting with anyone in the church. We should want them to hear the word preached and pray for them to be convicted by it. We should want them to engage with believers from the church who are calling them to repentance. In the end, church discipline is not primarily about getting rid of a terrible sinner who is beyond the pale; the goal is to bring a wandering brother or sister back to the Lord Jesus, encouraging them to repent of their sin so that they can be restored to the fellowship.

In the sad event that a person is removed from membership, it is important to say that they do not merely resign. Sometimes, an individual will resign their membership in a bid to avoid being publicly removed. The church should not allow this. Of course, the church can do nothing about a person writing a letter of resignation, nor can they stop a person from refusing to attend the church. These are all the prerogatives of the individual. But the church should not let a resignation letter stop them from asking the members to actively dismiss this person from membership. It is the duty of the members to determine who does and doesn't belong. It may seem like a formality when somebody has already written in to resign, but it is a formal declaration by the church to remove this person from membership and it says something about the role of the church when we receive a resignation letter from a person under discipline and, not merely accepting it, vote nevertheless to remove them from fellowship.

The other issue we can face when it comes to discipline is that of people coming to us from other churches. As a general rule of thumb, churches ought not to undermine the disciplinary process of another fellowship. In the normal run of things, I do not think churches should be accepting into membership those who are under discipline elsewhere. I say this tentatively – and am clear it is a general rule of thumb – because we cannot overlook the possibility this person has been unfairly dismissed from membership over an issue that our church would not agree warrants church discipline. If our church is of this opinion, we must be sure that we are not merely taking the individual's word for it. Proper investigation must take place. The church should make every effort to contact the other fellowship and find out exactly what has happened. It may be the person has been badly treated, but we should be slow to assume the worst of another church.

Chapter 21:

Members' Meetings

In the elder-led, member-ruled congregational model of church polity we have been outlining throughout this book, members' meetings are more vital than many want to admit. They can be viewed as cold, dusty meetings that are nothing more than a formality or as battlegrounds where all those vying for power and authority in the church butt heads; where members turn up to air their grievances against elders, who are seen only as jostling to control and quell the church. In short, a place where the very worst power dynamics are on full display. However, it really does not have to be this way!

When a church is functioning healthily, the members' meeting is the formal place where each part of the church exercises its God-given responsibilities. It is where the elders lead by laying out matters before the church and offering direction. It is where church finances are discussed: if the church is the vehicle for ministry, money is its fuel. At the members' meeting, members help shape what is done with the resources God has entrusted to them for the good of his kingdom. It is the place where members grasp hold of their duty to welcome new members, remove unrepentant ones and to appoint and remove their leaders, both elders and deacons. It is not a mere business meeting; it is a meeting of people on mission together working out what they are going to do to fulfil the objectives given to them by their commander-in-chief, the Lord Jesus Christ. It is a place where elders, deacons and members all have particular parts to play, particular responsibilities to shoulder, and where all work together to maximise their effectiveness in the gospel work of making and growing disciples. It is a place where the body of Christ acknowledges all its parts and plans how to exercise them for his glory.

With this biblical image in our minds again, let's look at the practicalities of these meetings and how we might come to look forward to, rather than dread, them.

Goal and Responsibilities

The goal of the members' meeting is to bring the whole church up to speed on their shared mission: to give the membership understanding of what the church has been doing, what the church will be doing and how they can embrace the mission of the church and play their part in it. The elders set the direction, the deacons have oversight of certain practical areas of church life, but it is the members who will necessarily be involved in fulfilling the mission. They need to understand why the church is doing what it does and why it is going to do what it will do. So it is important that, as far as possible, the whole church gathers for this. Every member has a part to play. There will be aspects of the meeting where they are to make a ruling – in matters pertaining to membership and appointment of leaders – but there will also be times when they are asked for their input to help inform the elders' thinking on a matter. There will similarly be times when they are required simply to listen to information – though free to ask clarifying questions – so that they can understand the mission of the church, the direction set by the elders and what may be required of them as they seek to fulfil it.

It is important for us to be clear who is responsible for what at the members' meeting. The Scriptures are the ultimate source of authority and the elders are to ensure everything is done in accord with them. The elders themselves are appointed to lead the church and so must assume that role. The deacons are tasked with ensuring the practical matters of ministry and church life are overseen and must update the church on their areas of responsibility. The members are to engage with the mission of the church and be aware of their responsibilities to accept and remove members and appoint and remove elders. They must be aware of the mechanisms for doing this and the elders must make provision for these things to take place.

Chairing and Agenda

In theory, anybody can chair a members' meeting. In practice, however, it makes most sense if one of the elders does it. This sets the right and proper framework of elders leading the church. For the same reason, the elders are the ones to set the agenda for a church members' meeting; much of the meeting will be given over to the elders raising matters before the church and giving their collective view on what is going to happen in relation to it. Ultimately, the elders will be laying before the members the matters that are pertinent to them and, as those appointed to lead the church, will be providing direction.

There is no reason a full-time elder must chair members' meetings. There may be practical reasons for it, but there is no scriptural reason they must. There is a good case for rotating the chair of the meeting between the elders. If, as we have been arguing, there is parity and equality amongst the eldership, this is demonstrated helpfully when different elders take the lead from the front. This is not to say it is wrong if – for any number of reasons – the full-time elder typically chairs members' meetings. Only, there is pragmatic value in rotating who chairs the meeting amongst the elders so that no one elder is viewed as above any of the others.

Some consider members' meetings the opportunity for members to 'really stick it to the elders'. There is absolutely nothing godly or biblical about this attitude. There should be nothing raised at a members' meeting that has not already been raised with the elders. If our concern is genuine, we will want to give our leaders a fair chance to consider and potentially act on whatever we want to raise. Ambushing leaders in the *Any Other Business* section with gripes and concerns that they haven't had time to think about won't lead to helpful change and is only likely to catch everyone off-guard.

Voting

Similarly, some consider that everyone should vote on everything all the time. After all, have we not argued that the Bible demonstrates congregational rule? But again, this attitude misses the point.

Members appoint their elders to lead and, once they have done so, agree to submit to their authority unless and until an elder disqualifies himself through serious, unrepentant sin. This means it is not the members' role to vote on everything. It is not the members' role to hold every decision of the elders – no matter what it may be – to account. Their job is to appoint their elders to lead and then submit to their authority in matters of church life. Members' meetings are not designed to be a direct democratic free-for-all, with votes on every matter. They are a place where elders lay out the direction of the church, where members may ask questions and have an opportunity for input, where the mission and its tactics are laid out and where the members may vote on matters over which God has specifically given them responsibility.

Some elders are fearful of dissenting voices in the church. But when members know that we love them, and we know they love us in turn, there is no reason to worry about such things. For this reason, it is my view that any votes taken in the church should not be private affairs. If members want to vote against a position recommended by the elders, it is almost certainly something the elders want to hear. For example, if a member knows that the person currently being considered for membership is living in sin – but this is unknown to the elders – this is something the church will want to hear rather than ignorantly voting such a person into membership. A secret ballot scotches any chance of finding these sorts of things out. Similarly, a private poll on an issue does nothing to help the church leadership understand *why* people disagree with them. By insisting on public voting, and people standing by their convictions publicly, the reasons for their decision-making can be heard. Elders who take their members seriously may decide to have a complete rethink based on the reasons given. If members know that elders will not reprimand them for disagreeing, and elders believe that members are genuinely seeking the good of the church, there is no reason to fear these sorts of disagreements. They should be received by the church leadership and considered in light of the reasons given, assuming the best motives of those bringing the objection.

Such disagreements can work to the good of the church. One of the key means of growth in the Christian life is in our dealings with other believers, particularly when they disagree with us. We all have to learn to deal patiently with one another. Sometimes we will have to submit to decisions that are not what we consider to be best. Allowing people to express their views openly and honestly is important in church life and elders should not be defensive when some of those voices are not entirely in line with their own. Sometimes the elders will be caused to rethink, other times the individual may simply have to submit to the elders or the collective will of the church. These are not problems to be avoided, but the inevitable results of people dealing with people and are best viewed as one of God's means of growing us into Christlike maturity. Naturally, the ideal situation in any members' meeting is to reach total unanimity. Nothing quite says unity as clearly as total and complete unforced agreement! Of course, unanimity is not always possible. Decisions nevertheless need to be made. Whilst no system will be perfect, this approach of listening to dissenting voices but then taking a majority decision means those who disagree can be properly heard and engaged with seriously whilst decision-making is not stymied by minority voices. That is to say, whilst unanimity is ideal, we are ultimately aiming to maintain unity even where we may disagree.

Deacons

Deacons have a crucial role at members' meetings. Often, though the elders may have steered a particular course, the deacons may well be the ones who are going to action matters. It can be particularly helpful when deacons have specific areas of responsibility in church life, and when they do, they will often be called upon to share updates at a members' meeting. So, the church treasurer will bring a financial report. The deacon for building maintenance may update the church about works undertaken on the facilities and highlight any areas that might need attention. Deacons with other roles might also be called to give an update on whatever practical area of church life they oversee. The contribution of the deacons in these things is vital. The elders will not have a day-to-day understanding of all the areas handled by the deacons; members may not know about or be involved in any or all of these things. The deacons will help the whole church understand the practical realities of church life.

Exercising the different parts of the body in making decisions

Whilst it is the duty of the elders to set the direction of the church, there are often times they may seek the collective wisdom of the deacons or the membership on a matter. Just as it is good household management to let your accountant wife oversee the finances in your home when maths is not a strong point for you, so it is foolish of elders to set themselves up as an authority in an area where they have no expertise while other members of the church do. Church members may have particular skills and knowledge that is lacking on the eldership. They may have experience from other churches about how particular decisions might develop unhelpfully. We are all shaped somewhat by our experiences and it is all too easy to let one bad experience colour our entire theology and practice in a given area. Elders do well to listen carefully to their members, to take their views and insights on board. However, ultimately the responsibility for church direction lies with them. That is, after all, what the church has appointed the elders to do.

Nevertheless, it is a foolish eldership who present their plans and conclusions – explaining their biblical rationale for it – then presses on with them in the face of serious opposition. This doesn't mean a small minority should hold the church to ransom. But if enough people – even a significant minority – are seriously pushing back on plans, it is sensible for the elders to listen. It may be appropriate to delay a decision whilst the concerns are weighed and evaluated. It may be that the elders need to sit down with the dissenting voices and work through the relevant Scriptures. It may be that the elders have missed something that these members have picked up on. Clifford Pond is surely right when he says, 'elders only earn the trust of the members if they are seen to take them seriously.'[1] Taking people seriously does not necessarily mean always agreeing with them or even doing an about turn on our plans. But at the very least it does mean listening to their concerns,

1 Pond, *Only Servants*, p.126

weighing them genuinely, perhaps taking them away for further discussion and, no doubt in some cases, changing course.

It should be the case then, in the ordinary run of things, that members accept and submit to the plans of the eldership. There will be times that members believe the elders direction and plans to be misguided or mistaken. There should be ample opportunity for members to make their representations to that effect. Elders, in turn, should listen to those raising concerns. Nevertheless, unless elders raise a matter for the first time in a members' meeting and ask for feedback, it is best (if the issue has been put on the agenda ahead of time) for members to bring their concern to the elders ahead of any meeting so they can think carefully about their response. It may be that they rethink the matter altogether. It may be that they disagree, but it pays to hear their considered view as to why, rather than a hot take. The input of members may be sought, but in the specific areas of responsibility given to elders their input may be advisory rather than binding. If the church maintains that its elders are qualified men, who have been appointed by the church to lead, the general disposition of the members ought to be in support of the elders unless they have strong and significant reasons to dissent. These reasons will always be heard more favourably if they come with genuine biblical principles that back them up.

All these things become so much less of an issue when we return to the image we started with: we are all members of a body, different and yet complementary to one another, functioning as one and yet not interchangeable. We are the body of Christ. He is our head, he is in charge, and he knows how we will best work together in a unity that nevertheless retains our individual differences. So, as we turn up at our church members' meeting, whatever our role, the very word 'membership' takes us back to the body with its varied and complementary parts. By God's design, we are always more, and never less, than the sum of our individual parts because we are joined together in one body under our head, the Lord Jesus Christ.

Chapter 22:

Elders, Teaching and Preaching

As we have seen earlier, one of the only skills demanded of elders in Scripture is the ability to teach. All the other eldership criteria concern character rather than ability. Whilst the eldership qualifications present a bottom line – the bare minimum for a man to be considered suitable – this one highlighted skill tells us that the ability to rightly handle the Scriptures and teach them to others is absolutely essential to what it means to be an elder.

Given the importance placed on this ability to teach for all elders, I do not think it is credible to differentiate teaching elders and ruling elders as some do. All elders must be able to teach. There is no get-out clause for those who simply bring their wisdom to elders' meetings but have no part to play in the teaching of the church. I fully accept 'able to teach' does not necessarily require every elder to be an A-grade preacher. But this qualification cannot mean less than it says: an elder must be able – in some forum in the life of the church – to teach. At a bare minimum, this means every elder should be able to understand the Scriptures and explain them clearly to another person. He may not be a great preacher, but he should be able to communicate Scripture, to defend sound doctrine and to lead others to understand the Bible, whether in the pulpit, group Bible study or on a one-to-one basis.

The importance of this for eldership cannot be overstated. If our churches are not being shaped by the word of God, they will be shaped by almost anything else. If the word is not the driving force in our churches, something else will drive us and, whatever it is, it won't be driving us in God's direction. Throughout the Old Testament, God led his people by his word. Jesus similarly told his disciples, '"Let's go on ... so that I may preach there too. This is why I have come"' (Mk. 1:38). Similarly, we see the early church committing themselves to the teaching of the Apostles (cf. Acts 2:42). That is, the teaching of Jesus they were tasked with passing on. The Apostles led through their teaching, which they received from Jesus. As we've already seen, the Apostles then gave way to local church elders who had devoted themselves to the Apostles' teaching, which is Jesus' teaching, and could pass it on. God led his people by the word, Jesus came to preach the word, the Apostles taught from the word and elders are tasked with leading by the word. What did Paul insist Timothy do in 2 Timothy 4:2? 'Preach the word; be ready in season and out of season; correct, rebuke, and encourage with great patience and teaching.' Indeed, if we understand Ephesians 4:11 to be speaking of one function when it says 'some pastors and teachers' (see Chapter 12), we must conclude that pastoring and teaching go together. That is to say, elders lead through teaching the word.

So, how is teaching to be delivered in the church? The primary point of teaching in the church will be a diet of weekly expository sermons. C.E.B. Cranfield, the former professor of theology at Durham University, said, 'The practice of preaching through biblical books section by section, in order, can be, I have long believed, if followed intelligently and sensitively, enormously beneficial to the church.'[1] Mark Dever writes:

> Expositional preaching is preaching in service to the Word [*sic*]. It presumes a belief in the authority of Scripture – that the Bible is actually God's Word; but it is something much more than that. A commitment to expositional preaching is a commitment to *hear* God's Word – not just to affirm that it is God's Word but to submit to it ... Christian preachers today have authority to speak from God only so long as they speak his message and unfold his words ... they are not commanded simply to go and preach. They are commanded specifically to go and preach the Word.[2]

Behind systematic expositional preaching lies a belief that the whole of God's word is relevant to God's people all of the time. It insists that passages are to be understood in the context in which they were given. It wants the main point of a passage to be the main point of the sermon. It does not want to preach topically according to whatever the elders think the church might need to

1 As quoted in Dever, *Nine Marks*, p.56

2 Ibid., p.44

hear, but wants God himself to set the agenda and for the church to be shaped by whatever he wants them to hear.

While there is no requirement for all elders to be excellent preachers, an inability to convey what a passage means and apply it to a congregation from the pulpit may well evidence an inability to teach. Elders need not necessarily be preachers, in the sense that they may lack the soft skills required to communicate well in a 40-minute sermon. Some are simply more boring than others. Some may not communicate well in that setting but do better in a Bible study. But I have not yet met a truly qualified elder who is unable to convey basic doctrine or the meaning of a passage at all. Elders need to be able to maintain biblical doctrine, handle the Scriptures adequately and explain them to some degree. They don't have to be someone under whose preaching you would want to sit consistently but they must clearly understand and apply the Scriptures and hold faithfully to biblical doctrine. If they can't demonstrate that ability in the pulpit, it is reasonable to question whether they have the ability at all.

Whilst the word of God is always relevant to God's people, sadly the application of God's word by many preachers often isn't. Not only must preaching make the meaning of Scripture understandable to the average hearer, but those same Scriptures should be meaningfully applied to the hearers' lives. We shouldn't use tired illustrations that mean nothing to modern-day people. We shouldn't fight yesterday's theological, social or cultural battles in the pulpit when modern life and most churches have long since moved on. We recognise the unchanging nature of God's word, but we must nevertheless recognise the changing nature of the world around us. The goal of expositional preaching is to preach the old truths and apply them to current contexts. The word of God doesn't change but people do; their cultures, contexts and churches are necessarily different to the world of the biblical writers who themselves were not all writing into the same cultural contexts. Moses, for example, was not writing into the same context as Paul. Old truths need to be applied in fresh ways.

Alongside regular expository preaching, the church may provide other opportunities to engage with the word. The following means are, I believe, helpful in the teaching of the local church. However, none are *demanded* of local churches. Scripture commands those who teach to preach the word. Preaching is the only mandated form of teaching in Scripture. All these other means are, therefore, potentially beneficial but not something we can or should mandate for everyone.

It is common for churches to host home groups. At their best, these groups provide accountability for church members, time to share individual prayer needs and to pray for the mission of the church, and teaching from the word. Whilst I do not believe elders necessarily have to lead home groups, it is a matter of wisdom to have an elder present where possible. Moreover, if an elder is not regularly involved in preaching the word – perhaps they are an unpaid elder in secular work with less time than the paid pastor – it may be more important for him to exercise his ability to teach through the home group.

For the most part, the teaching that takes place in home groups is likely to be discussion-based. That doesn't mean – as some are wont to argue – that whoever is leading is simply 'floating questions' for people to discuss. Many, even some complementarians, have argued in favour of women leading these meetings in mixed-sex settings on the basis that they aren't teaching but merely 'facilitating discussion'. I think this view is problematic. A good home group leader is not merely floating questions. They are listening to answers, challenging people to think carefully, drawing out proper conclusions and correcting error where it arises. They are doing much more than facilitating a free discussion; they are actively engaged in a form of teaching. They do not simply accept any given answer as legitimate but continually point back to the Scriptures and shape the discussion so that people are led to biblical conclusions. They are purposefully teaching from the Scriptures socratically, i.e. the aim is to teach, not merely discuss. Nor can we suggest that home groups are not part of the formal teaching of the church when they are established by the church for the purpose of teaching the Bible. If they are an extension of the church's formal teaching, it is important that someone who is qualified and recognised as able to teach takes a lead in these meetings. As such, having an elder to lead – or at least in the group overseeing what teaching is taking place – makes sense.

In my church, further to the above, we hold a weekly Theology Breakfast. Though all expository sermons will contain theology and doctrine, there is often a gap in the knowledge of many churchgoers. They hear sermons week by week, they may even pick up how to handle a passage of Scripture over time because of this, but there is often little in the way of specific doctrinal input. To meet this need, for an hour before the Sunday morning service, we run a theological Bible study. In that study, over the course of two years, we run through a curriculum of basic systematic theology, biblical theology, historical theology, Bible exposition and ecclesiology. Our aim in this is to build up the members in their knowledge of God and his word in a way that sermons are unlikely to do. Again, this is an excellent opportunity for an elder to be involved in the teaching programme of the church.

Beyond this, there are one-to-one opportunities for discipleship. Every member of the church can read the Bible with one another. But they are only likely to do this when elders are doing it themselves. Forming discipleship relationships within the church is another way elders can exercise their ability to teach. Simply sitting down with members of the church and reading the Bible together, or engaging with the theology in a helpful Christian book, is a cause of real growth within the church and a good vehicle for elders to exercise a teaching ministry outside the pulpit.

In all these things, the goal is to help people understand the Scriptures. These are all vehicles through which elders can exercise their ability to teach. An ability to teach is only properly recognised when the people you are teaching are actually learning. If they're not learning, you aren't teaching. If you can't do it any other way, then you are not able to teach. Which means teaching and preaching within the church must be understandable. It must be accessible. It must be capable of being understood by the average person in the church. We are aiming to make God's word clear to God's people and to help them understand what they have to do, think or believe in response to it. That is, fundamentally, what teaching is and it is demanded of every elder in the church.

We may have all these fine means of teaching in our church and yet still find our teaching is ineffective. Tim Keller once tweeted, 'In large churches, people let you pastor [because] of your preaching. In small churches, people let you preach [because] of your pastoring generally.'[3] One of the reasons why our preaching may be ineffective is because of our approach to pastoring more generally. One pastor once said, 'if people know that you love them you can say anything to them.' If our people do not know that we love them, our preaching and teaching is likely to be ineffective. Whilst all elders are called to teach the congregation, and to lead by teaching, they are also called to love the church. Unless people know that we love them, they are unlikely to want to hear the hard truths of God's word from us. If we are preaching with conviction for conviction, we must love our people and they must know we love them if they are going to respond to anything that leaves our mouths. Our people need to trust us if they are going to listen to us.

An important aspect of earning the trust of those under our care is authenticity. If people sense you are not yourself, they will soon wonder what, exactly, you are hiding. One of the problems with a lot of traditional church preaching is that it tries to force people into a uniform cultural mould. Not only are the clothes the man wears on a Sunday nothing like what he would wear throughout the week, but his style of speaking is different and his mannerisms seem affected. If you spoke to him after the meeting, it could seem like you were dealing with two different people. Preaching like this

---

3 Keller, T., Twitter post, 17th August 2022, accessed at https://twitter.com/timkellernyc/status/1559970936740364288?lang=en, accessed 08/09/2025

is likely to be ineffective because it is not authentic. If you are a jeans and hoodie kind of person, that is the person you should be in the pulpit. If you are a suit and tie kind of person ordinarily, be that person in the pulpit. The same goes for our personalities. We ought to be the same people in the pulpit as we are out of it, the same people in our teaching as we are when we are just hanging out. People will quickly see through a fraud and, understandably, not want to listen to them because they can't be trusted. Our style of speech, our personality, the way we engage with people should be authentic and honest.

Clifford Pond argues that 'provision should be made for our congregation to say if they have understood our preaching, and what they have understood us to say.'[4] I agree. It has been our practice as a church to use our midweek home groups for exactly this purpose. The same passage that is preached on Sunday will be read again midweek. A brief two-minute overview of the sermon is given. Then, there is opportunity for anyone in the group to ask any questions they may have or offer any particular insights they gleaned. Once people have shared, the questions all focus on the particular applications of the sermon. We use the home groups to push people to think more pointedly about what the word means for them in their situations. I understand Tim Keller used to invite people to the front after every sermon so they could ask him any questions they had of the passage that was just preached. Similarly, Clifford Pond says, 'Some of my most challenging and yet rewarding experiences have been when I have gathered the people after a service and asked them to tell me what they had understood me

4 Pond, *Only Servants*, p.140

to say, what they had not understood, and how they would apply the message to themselves.'[5] However you do it – and there is no one legitimate way – gauging whether our people have actually understood, and what they have understood, is vitally important.

In all of our efforts to teach, we must be clear why any of it matters to the people we are speaking with. Unless the preacher makes clear why any of what he is saying matters, nobody is likely to listen. On top of showing why it matters, we must be careful in our teaching not to get sidetracked by 'interesting details'. I put that in quotes because, let's be honest, they almost never are! They are more aptly described as 'things the preacher found interesting in their study but nobody else will'! We have to be ruthless with our material, not including everything we could possibly say about the passage, but highlighting the main point and showing why it matters for the people listening. Anybody who spends half their sermon talking about the historical context of a city mentioned or the flora and fauna of the geographical region has already lost the overwhelming majority of their congregation. Do people really need to know this? Is this vital to understanding what this passage is about? Will this information do anything for the needy souls listening? These are the questions we must ask of our preaching and teaching. Simple and straightforward is always better than wordy explanation.

Elderships ought to think through the teaching programmes of the church together. Whether it is what series to do next at Sunday meetings, how to organise home groups or whatever other modes of teaching might be appropriate, all the elders should be involved

5 Ibid., p.40

in working out teaching programmes. It might be, for practical reasons, one particular elder takes a lead in this area, but he should come back to the eldership with his proposals and suggestions, explaining what he thinks would be good and hearing from his fellow elders. Between them, the elders should be seeking to teach the whole counsel of God and all of the elders ought to be actively involved in some way in word ministry.

Chapter 23:

Training and Sending

We have seen already that the fundamental task of elders is to equip the saints for works of service. They are to teach and train people through the word to be disciple-making disciples. This all means there is, built into the job description, a need for elders to train and send workers. Workers are to be trained for work in their own local church and to be sent where needed to bless and build up other local churches.

Training

All too often, churches delegate their responsibility to train their people to outside colleges and, in some contexts, para-church organisations. Do not misunderstand me when I say this is not good. Bible colleges can often provide what local churches cannot in the way of certain kinds of training. There is nothing wrong with tapping into these resources as a local church and actively sending your people there. However, I think churches all too often jump straight to outside providers without doing the hard work of in-context training that they are called to do. Whilst Bible colleges may supplement local church training in various ways, it is the duty of local church elders to provide meaningful training to their members. That is, after all, what discipleship means! It is discipline in training.

Training in the local church takes many forms. Lest we forget, Sunday meetings – with all their various ways of serving the church among the members – and the preaching of the word are key means of training God's people in righteousness. We often overlook sermons and the ordinary, regular meetings with God's people, but these are biblical, God-ordained means of growing in our knowledge and love for the Lord Jesus Christ. Which one of us would countenance sending a person who aspired to be an elder, pastor, missionary or indeed to enter any other form of full-time Christian service and yet had no interest in the Sunday gathering of God's people, in serving in it and learning from it? It cannot be said enough: Sunday meetings are the primary, God-ordained means of growth in maturity and training for Christian service.

Sunday sermons alone are not enough, however. Whilst we wholeheartedly believe in the preaching of the word on a Sunday, many seem to believe this alone will suffice. But as Payne and Marshall point out, 'Sunday sermons are necessary but not sufficient ... Sermons are needed, yes, but they are not *all* that is needed.'[1] The fact is, our sermons cannot do everything. No doubt consistent, faithful, biblical, weekly preaching can achieve a lot – often a lot more than we credit. But it can't do everything. You can

1 Payne & Marshall, *Trellis & Vine*, p.102

preach amazing sermons on the importance of evangelism, but unless someone is looking for and taking evangelistic opportunities, they will never grow in this area. No doctor trains for medicine by spending five years in the classroom and never once dealing with an actual patient. In the same way, we don't train evangelists, missionaries, pastors and planters through sermons alone. This is only one part of training.

As already mentioned, our church aims to fill the notable theological gap in our churches with a weekly Theology Breakfast: a Bible study looking at key biblical and theological ideas. The aim is to offer the whole church a basic grounding in systematic, biblical and historical theology – including a biblical understanding of what the church and proper church order is – alongside teaching them to read the Bible for themselves. Anyone is welcome to come but the purpose is simple: to supplement the regular preaching of the word with an underpinning in theology. One of the effects of doing this has been to see people picking up on themes we have discussed in the Theology Breakfast when they hear them in sermons. Theological connections are made and lights seem to go on.

Further, we have regular home groups that look into the Scriptures together. We typically take the sermon that was preached on Sunday and press into its applications more deeply. This has the two-fold benefit of re-emphasising the word as preached on Sunday and applying the word more clearly to the specific situations of those in the group. Beyond this, it encourages members to think about how to apply the Scriptures appropriately and it models right handling of the word.

Similarly, as part of our regular diet, we encourage our members to read good Christian books. We do this in three ways. First, we have links on our website to useful resources that anyone can click on, find a helpful book and buy it for themselves. Second, we have a book stall in the church building that sells books at a reduced rate. This also gives people the opportunity to request resources we don't have and to receive recommendations from others. Third, as part of our weekly service, we do book giveaways. We want people to engage with good theology and so we give them good material. Even if they don't read it, over time, they learn about good authors who are theologically dependable, they hear just in the titles of books the theological things we think matter and they see that we are committed to ministry that is word-based and theologically grounded. If they read them, they get much more out of them still.

Alongside these things, we want to encourage discipling relationships amongst our members: older members meeting with younger members, more mature members meeting with newer converts, to discuss the Scriptures. Part of the reason for giving away books is so discipling relationships can develop. Books and study notes are the fodder of discipling relationships. We want people to meet up, having read the same book and engaged the same Scriptures, and hold each other to account. We want them to help each other grow in maturity, challenging where needed and encouraging where appropriate. Through these things, we think people will grow. They will grow in their knowledge and love of the Lord Jesus, in their understanding of the Scriptures and in their relational skills with others.

These things might all be considered matters of 'building up': they require input from one person in order to help another grow. But we also need to provide in-context opportunities to serve. Alongside these means of building up the body through discipleship, we want to provide opportunities for members to go out and make disciples. The best way to grow as a disciple-maker is to go and start making some disciples!

The church that is all action and no learning may well have great community relations but it will be theologically shallow. The church that is all learning and no action may well have great head knowledge but will inhibit their growth, both numerically and qualitatively, by failing to go where Jesus calls them. To train our people adequately we need both. We need opportunities to learn from the Scriptures and imitate godly role models whilst simultaneously being moved to action and serving in the things Jesus has called us to serve in.

If we are going to train people, then we need to make provision for them to train. We need to actually let others organise and lead. If we want to raise up preachers, having given them the appropriate theological input, we need to give them the opportunity to preach. To raise up evangelists, having given them proper support, they need opportunities to actually share the gospel with unbelievers. Part of building up in knowledge and maturity must include giving people opportunities to put what they have learnt into practice.

Sending

If the work of training members is happening as it ought, it is likely churches will also be called upon to send workers to support other churches or into other areas of ministry. This could mean sending out missionaries to unreached people, planting new churches in forgotten parts of a country or sending out pastors to serve in other, established congregations. In Acts 16:1–4, this is exactly what we see the church in Lystra do with Timothy. He was a well-regarded member of the church who was suitable to send with Paul on his missionary journey. This is similar to Paul and Barnabas being sent from the church in Antioch (cf. Acts 13:1–3). The early church clearly saw the value of training and then sending out workers for the sake of the gospel.

Elders of local churches need to be intentional about this sort of training. The fact is, it is evangelistic churches that tend to produce evangelists, Bible-focused churches that produce Bible teachers, mission-minded churches that produce missionaries. If we want to see all these kinds of people raised up within the church and sent out for the kingdom, then our churches have to be places where these things are seen to be important. There have to be opportunities for people to meaningfully engage in these things.

Discerning whether to go into a ministry role – whatever that might be – can happen in a number of ways. An individual may have a desire to go into a particular area of gospel ministry and speak to their elders about it. The church may recognise certain skills and competencies in a person and seek to encourage them towards ministry. It may even be believers from outside the church that prompt either the individual or the elders to begin thinking about a person this way. There is no one biblical means of discerning suitable people to send.

What is clear is that there is no call unless it is apparent to the church sending and the one calling as well as to the individual.

Someone might have a burning desire to go and reach a particular country, but if the sending church have seen no evidence of evangelistic zeal locally, how can they commend that person? For this reason, a person must be tested in their own church before being sent anywhere else. This is never more appropriate than when it comes to preaching. All too often, churches farm out their trainee preachers to smaller congregations, while refusing to let them anywhere near their own pulpit. This is wrong. If they are not okay to serve in your pulpit, they are not okay to serve a smaller congregation. A person should be trained in their own church and tested amongst people who know them before they are sent out. We have no business sending anyone that we have not seen serving in our own church, whom we have not seen in action and cannot positively commend. True calling will be the coming-together of three things: a desire to do the ministry on the part of an individual, a commendation by the sending church that this person is suitable and an actual call from a receiving church. It is inappropriate to send in the absence of any one of these.

If the church is sending a worker to a receiving church, it is good for the receiving church to take ownership of pastoral care. A church is limited in what support it can provide from a distance, so it makes much more sense for the local congregation where the worker is physically present to support them in their day-to-day ministry. However, not every worker is sent into a situation where this is possible. Where someone is going out to plant a new church or is being sent into mission work in an unevangelised part of the world, pastoral care will necessarily be in the hands of the sending church. Of course, if there are mission agencies involved who are helping to facilitate the local church sending, there will be means of support to access here. However, as a general rule, receiving churches should take responsibility for pastoral care and sending churches should do so only if and when there is no receiving church to speak of.

Chapter 24:

Prayer

Prayer is vitally important in the life of the local church. In Acts 2:42, prayer is one of the four foundational things to which the early church devoted themselves. In 1 Thessalonians 5:17, Paul instructs the local church simply: 'pray constantly'. Elders are, of course, to lead the church through teaching but they are also called to the ministry of prayer. The reason for this is obvious enough. Psalm 127:1 clearly states: 'Unless the Lord builds a house, its builders labour over it in vain; unless the Lord watches over a city, the watchman stays alert in vain.' The ministry of the local church belongs, start to finish, to the Lord. Unless he is involved in every aspect of church life our efforts will be meaningless. We show our dependence on God, we seek his will and we demonstrate our belief in his power to work for his glory and our good by submitting to him in prayer.

Just like the regular preaching of the word, one key way we will encourage our members to be praying people is through the regular church prayer meeting. This is not the only space for prayer in the life of the church, but it is a helpful means of encouraging our people to pray. It is in the prayer meeting that our people learn *how* to pray. As newer believers hear older saints praying to God, giving thanks to him, seeking his will, praying for him to work, they will learn to pray themselves. When his disciples asked Jesus to teach them how to pray, he taught them by praying (cf. Lk. 11:1). On that same basis, elders and mature believers in the church can help church members to pray simply by praying with them. It is by hearing and imitating the prayers of God's people that others are trained to pray. For this reason, the prayer meeting is a training ground of prayer warriors.

In our church, we also have a weekly time of open prayer as part of our regular Sunday worship. We allow anybody in the church the opportunity to pray during the service. We preach near the front end, and all that happens thereafter is supposed to be a response to the word. We are actively encouraging our people, in the time of prayer, to pray in response to the word. As people do so, younger believers hear older believers pray and can imitate their prayers. They are taught to pray by hearing others.

Alongside public prayer, elders' meetings should be bathed in prayer. At our own elders' meetings, we have three points in our meeting where we pray. One of us will pray for God to guide us by his Spirit as we discuss the matters of the church. Partway through our meeting we then share personal needs and pray for one another as elders. Finally, at the end of our meeting, we pray through all the points and matters that have been discussed in that meeting, praying for each individually. This isn't just a weekly ritual we have fallen into; it is born of a genuine desire for Jesus to work in our church for his glory. In John 15:5 Jesus says, 'you can do nothing without me.' We are so conscious that we are unable to do anything of ourselves. This being true, what fools we are if we neglect prayer! As elders dependent on the Lord, we pray at every elders' meeting: for the meeting itself, for one another and then for the specifics of church life that have been under discussion.

Elders should also be constantly encouraging personal, private prayer outside of formal meetings. They should be encouraging prayer amongst the members for the work of ministry. They should be encouraging the church to pray for one another, particularly the needs among the congregation. They should be encouraging the church to pray for their elders to be effective in the work they have been given to do. Prayer ought to permeate the life of the church. Nothing will encourage our members to do this more than seeing their elders do it: elders praying with members of the church for personal matters, for God's will to be revealed, for the promises of the word to be applied in the lives of those we are praying with. Elders model personal and private prayer in this way and encourage their members to pray for the church along with them.

Other opportunities to pray may be scattered throughout the life of the church. In home groups we make sure we pray for one another. The benefit of this is that more timid members, who might be too shy or scared to pray in a Sunday meeting, may feel more comfortable doing so in the intimacy of a smaller group. But again, the goal of praying for one another in the home group is to encourage the membership to be praying for one another. They can do that once per week in the group, but it should also encourage them to be thinking about and praying for one another much more regularly.

Elders need to model helpful forms of praying in the life of the church. Far too many meetings suffer from the belief that God will hear us because of our many words. We know it was not genuine believers Jesus was calling out when he said that (Mt. 6:7). Yet many of our prayer meetings are deeply off-putting to people because many prattle on, saying very little, in as many words as possible. Elders need to be alive to this sort of thing and encourage those who would pray simple and straightforward prayers. They must model that it is okay to pray short, succinct prayers. God does not hear us because of the number of words we use.

Similarly, elders should model the range and breadth of prayer. Clifford Pond says, 'prayer meetings sometimes become rather feeble. We are given a list of needs of members or of others in whom the church has an interest. We deliver our "shopping list" and then go home ... there are notes missing in such prayer meetings to the loss of the church.'[1] There is, of course, nothing wrong with bringing our needs before the Lord. Jesus encourages us to ask our Heavenly Father for good things. But so often that is all we do. There is often little room for praise and worship of the Lord himself. We must model in our churches the full breadth and range of prayers. Our prayers should often focus less on us and our needs and more on God and who he is. There should well be less asking and more thanksgiving. There is much we can pray for and about and our prayer life is lacking if it mainly consists of prayers about our health and temporal concerns. In the end, there is more to prayer than just asking God for stuff. Elders need to make sure there is space for us to do other things and to model what they are.

1 Pond, *Only Servants*, p.148

When we are praying for wants and needs, our prayers ought to reflect the priorities of God. When we pray about the ministry, we ought to be encouraging kingdom-minded prayers. We are not looking to see our empire built and our numbers swell, we are looking for spiritually dead people to be brought to new life in Christ, whether that redounds to the glory of our church or not. We are looking to see God's people built up in the faith and grown to maturity in Christ. We are looking for the gospel to go out in our community and are asking God, not only to give us opportunities to share the gospel, but to go before us and prepare hearts that are ready by the Holy Spirit to receive the Lord Jesus. Rather than constant prayers for Mabel's knee and Phil's dodgy back, John's job and Alice's family concern, we should be praying prayers that reflect God's priorities. That isn't to say these things don't matter to the Lord, or that they shouldn't matter to us, but our prayer life is often dominated by them. When we do pray for such things, our priorities do not always reflect God's priorities. We find ourselves only asking for relief from these sorts of difficulties rather than asking God to glorify himself through our circumstances. That may mean healing us or it may mean bringing him more glory by our patient suffering and continued belief in his goodness despite difficult circumstances. Elders do well to lead their churches to pray for the things that God would have them pray about and to pray for the things he would give them.

This is no small thing. Underlying our prayers are implicit theological assumptions. There are good assumptions, so the very act of praying suggests there is a sovereign God who is able and willing to work for our good. But there are often bad assumptions, so continual prayers for healing and more comfortable living situations may come from an understanding rooted in Prosperity Gospel thinking. We would never say that coming to Jesus means resolving all our problems in this life, but our prayers often reveal that we kind of think it will. Again, that is not to say it is wrong to ever pray for these things. Paul prayed for his thorn in the flesh to be removed three times (cf. 2 Cor. 12:7–9), so he clearly knew God could act in this way, wanted God to intervene and knew it was OK to ask for it. Note, however, that Paul prayed three times and when it became clear God was not going to remove it, and this was so that he would actually experience God's grace more fully, Paul stopped praying about it. There was no assumption that God always wanted him to be healthy, wealthy and comfortable. Rather, there was a belief in the goodness of God who would work all things to his own glory and for Paul's ultimate good. Very often, our prayers do not reflect that sort of thinking and belie our otherwise sound theology. Elders need to lead their churches to pray in ways that are scriptural and reflect the priorities of Jesus Christ for his church.

Chapter 25:

Member Relationships

Mark Dever insists 'The responsibilities and duties of members of a Christian church are simply the responsibilities and duties of Christians.'[1] The Oldham Bethel Church Membership Handbook lays out those general responsibilities and duties this way:

> Church members, just like all Christian people, are called to be baptised (Act 2:38) and regularly partake of the Lord's Supper (Act 2:42). They are to hear and obey God's Word [*sic*] (Rom 2:13; Jam 1:22). They are to meet together for fellowship and build one another up (Heb 10:24f). They are to love God (Luk 10:27), one another (Joh 13:34f) and those outside the church (Jud 1:22f; 1Pe 2:17; 1Ti 2:1). They are to evidence the fruit of the Spirit in their lives (Gal 5:22f) and glorify God in all the activities

1 Dever, *Nine Marks*, p.159

> of their life whether at home, work, in the community or anywhere else (Rom 12:1; 1Co 10:31).[2]

But Scripture also details specific duties of members to one another as well as their duties and responsibilities towards their elders. Again, the Oldham Bethel Church Membership Handbook outlines them this way:

> **Duties to other members**: love one another (John 13:34f; Rom 12:10; Gal 5:14); seek peace and unity (Rom 12:16; 14:19; 1Th 5:13); avoid strife and discord (2Co 13:11; Php 2:1-3); care for one another (Gal 6:10; Heb 13:6; Jam 1:27; 1Jo 3:17); keep each other accountable (Gal 6:1f; 2Th 3:15; Heb 12:15); edify each other (1Th 5:11; 1Pe 4:10); bear with each other (Mat 18:21f; Mar 11:25; Rom 15:1; Gal 6:2); pray for each other (Eph 6:18; Jam 5:16); avoid those who would destroy the church (Rom 16:17; Tit 3:10; 2Jo 1:10-11); contend for the gospel (Php 1:27; Jud 1:3); act as examples to each other (Php 2:1-18).
>
> **Duties to leaders**: respect and honour their leaders (Php 2:29; 1Th 5:12f; 1Ti 5:17); obey and submit to their leaders (Heb 13:17); believe and defend their church leaders against accusation (1Ti 5:19); imitate their leaders (1Co 4:16, 11:1; Heb 13:7); financially support their leaders (1Ti 5:17; 1Co 9:7-14; Gal 6:6); pray for their leaders (Col 4:3f; 2Th 3:1; Heb 13:18f).[3]

---

2 Membership Handbook, pp.14-15

3 Ibid., p.15

But there are two opposite extremes that churches can fall into in terms of how members treat their elders. The first is putting leaders on pedestals and treating them as if they can do no wrong. This is incredibly dangerous both for the man and the church. At a bare minimum, it tempts elders to pride. In the worst cases, it leads to a cultic church, where the elders brook no dissent and consider themselves infallible. This is even worse if the model of church polity gives a single elder greater authority than the others. It places one man above them all and he can end up acting like a demigod: any questioning of his authority, deviation from his vision or differences between him and the congregation are viewed as tantamount to standing against God himself. It is not healthy for anyone.

The other danger is for members to treat their leaders with contempt and refuse to recognise their authority at all. In these circumstances, elders can't do right for doing wrong. Members constantly criticise, actively undermining the elders at every turn, stir up dissent amongst the membership and create an atmosphere in which it is almost impossible for the church to be effective and fruitful. There is nothing godly in these sorts of attitudes either.

Both of these stances towards church elders are deeply unhelpful. As John Benton says, 'The future of the churches will not be served by the straightjacket of fear brought about by domineering leaders and condemnatory congregations ... The future of the churches must be laid in love.'[4] As members, that love must be seen in a supportive attitude towards the elders we have appointed to serve us. Such love includes respect and honour

4 Benton, *Balanced Pastor*, p.105

towards our leaders, obedience and submission, assuming the best of the elders – particularly in the face of accusations – financial support for those who labour full-time in ministry and, perhaps most importantly of all, praying for our leaders. These are the biblical commands to members in relation to their leaders that we listed above. This is how members show their love for their leaders.

This is a thoroughly biblical principle. Jesus, when speaking to his disciples in John 14, tells them: 'if you love me, you will keep my commands' (v15). Jesus wants us to really grasp this point because he says it in some form four times in the chapter. The disciples of Christ will demonstrate their love for him by obeying his commands. This is something Jesus does himself. In the same chapter he says, 'so that the world may know that I love the Father, I do as the Father commanded me' (v31). Jesus demonstrates his own love for the Father by keeping his commands. Where God has established order and relational authority, there are right and proper ways to love one another. Love is demonstrated by the one in authority serving the needs of those under them while those under their care demonstrate their love by obedience and submission to the one in authority. So, it seems reasonable – particularly when we read Hebrews 13:17 – to say that church members most meaningfully demonstrate their love for their elders by submitting to them and obeying their instruction. This is how Jesus demonstrates his love for the Father and how his disciples demonstrate their love for Jesus. If it's okay for Jesus and doesn't diminish him, it should be okay for us and won't diminish us.

Of course, this sort of authority and submission is not supposed to be servile. The Son is not subordinate to the Father. Yet, in

Gethsemane, Jesus submitted his human will to the divine will of Father, Son and Holy Spirit. This is similar to marriage, where a wife submits to her husband: it's not obsequious, mindless obedience, but rather an affectionate acceptance of headship whereby her husband is called to love her as Christ loved the church and she submits to him as he denies himself for her sake. A godly husband wants his wife to bring all of her gifts, skills and intelligence to family life so that all members of the family may flourish. She doesn't overlook his faults but seeks to help her husband overcome them. She doesn't make herself less clever or competent in order to avoid bruising his ego. Loving submission, in the context of a marriage that is seeking to help each partner flourish to the fullest, involves servant leadership that imitates Jesus and godly submission modelled on the church. Ephesians 5:32 couldn't be clearer: marriage is designed to be a picture of the mutual love between Christ and the church. Just as Christ loved the church and gave himself for her, elders are to give themselves in love to the leadership of their churches – loving the members with the same love with which Christ has loved his church – and members are to submit to elders, as they would submit to the Lord, knowing that the elders are his under-shepherds gifted to the church by him for their good (cf. Eph. 4:11; Heb. 13:17; 1 Pet. 5:1–4). It is a loving relationship, vested with God-ordained authority, for the purpose of all parts of the church flourishing to the full. In such a church, domineering leadership has no place and disdain for leadership plays no part.

So, what does respect and submission within the church look like in practice? Clifford Pond says, 'If members recognise the validity of the work elders do they will not behave as though the elders do not exist.'[5] This means members will seek the counsel of their elders and value the advice given. At the same time, there is a balance to be struck. Elders will not be so controlling that they insist every aspect of a person's life must be brought to them for their approval. John Benton points out that, 'God's word does not specify everything down to the last detail. It delineates a bounded space of right belief and behaviour. But within that space Christians have freedom (Jn. 8:31-32). Thus, there are areas in which Christians are at liberty to think for themselves and even take different points of view. This is to be respected by leaders.'[6]

Members who respect their leaders will also not gossip about them. As we have said already, that doesn't mean we should be blind to the faults of our elders. But it does mean that we will think before we criticise, and ask ourselves the question, 'Why am I telling this particular person about that specific issue?' Love demands that we do not gossip about our leaders but instead, where there are issues, we speak to them directly. Wisdom suggests that criticising our leaders in front of our friends and neighbours is unlikely to draw them to Christ or the church. It is neither loving our leaders nor our friends and neighbours well to do this. In our own family homes, just as constantly criticising our leaders is unlikely to help our children love the church, so pretending things are great when there are issues does not help our children love the church either. Our families have eyes and ears, and it is gaslighting to pretend things are great when we all know they are not. However, if we

5 Pond, *Only Servants*, p.152

6 Benton, *Balanced Pastor*, p.26

really love and respect our leaders, we will assume positive intent. Whatever criticism we may make, we will assume the very best even if what is going on is less than excellent and, if we love the church, we will seek to resolve the issues in godly ways.

Similarly, respect and honour for our leaders will translate into meaningful support for them. In 1 Timothy 5:17–18 Paul says, 'The elders who are good leaders are to be considered worthy of double honour, especially those who work hard at preaching and teaching. For the Scripture says: Do not muzzle an ox while it is treading out the grain, and, "The worker is worthy of his wages."' It is almost certain Paul is thinking about financial recompense here. He links honour with a command about oxen being permitted to eat grain whilst working – even animals should be rewarded for their work – and, more pointedly, with the fact that workers are worthy of their wages. We cannot avoid Paul's use of the phrase 'those who *work* hard at preaching and teaching' (my emphasis). The reference to workers being worthy of their wages seems pointedly linked to workers labouring in preaching and teaching. At a minimum, it seems a strange view of honour – and even more so double honour – to insist on keeping pastors poor. Paul's specific link to wages and rewards, even for animals working, suggests double honour has something to do with financial support for elders who labour in word-ministry. This links with 1 Corinthians 9:6 where Paul intimates, despite the choice he and Barnabas have made not to receive support, that other gospel workers are legitimately and rightly financially supported.

In practice, members who respect and honour their elders will ensure their needs are met. As we have already mentioned in earlier chapters, sometimes a pastor's wife may work. If a church wants to free up both a pastor and his wife for full-time ministry, they should be prepared to pay for that privilege. If it is not 'double honour' to keep a pastor's salary low to begin with, what should we say about paying a pastor a paltry salary and then expecting a two-for-the-price-of-one deal with his wife thrown in for free? It is deeply insulting. Similarly, if a church expects a pastor to live at a certain wage, considering it appropriate for him, individuals must ask themselves – if they are earning considerably more than that – why they are not giving the excess to the church. It is wholly inappropriate to insist on a salary point for a pastor, and determine that is fine for him and his family, whilst insisting you couldn't possibly live by such means. This is failing to show 'double honour' and is neither honest nor selfless. Some churches will insist on matching a salary to a comparable secular role, linking it to the teacher's scale for example.[7] Whilst there may be good reasons to do this, churches must make sure that if that is the principle they are operating on, then it really is a scale. If your pastor begins on the starting salary for a newly qualified teacher, something has gone awry if, ten years into his pastorate, he remains at the same point on the scale. A scale, by its nature, goes up with experience and there are opportunities for increase in salary by taking on greater responsibility. If we really are salary-matching, we must actually match the scale rather than pay lip-service to it.

7 While pay scales and salary expectations differ from culture to culture, the principle articulated here still stands. There is a clear mandate in Scripture for churches to support their pastors as generously as possible, providing for their needs and helping finance to not be a distraction from ministry.

Whilst some still insist that if they keep the pastor poor he will work harder, Clifford Pond strongly objects: 'This was not only immoral it was ineffective. If you starve the ox it will not work! But if you relieve full-time men from more than normal concern about "making ends meet" you will then release them for prayer, the study of the word, pastoral ministry and the relaxation to which all are entitled.'[8] When full-time elders are properly respected and honoured this way, it is a real encouragement to them. How we spend our money is some measure of what we truly value. If we are really putting our money where our mouths are when it comes to word-ministry, it is a real encouragement to the one labouring hard on our behalf to faithfully bring us the word of God.

Of course, encouragement extends well beyond money. It isn't less than financial support, but it is certainly more than it. You could pay your full-time elder a six-figure salary but, if you clearly hold him in contempt and treat him like your lackey, if you make demands on his family and treat them with disdain, there is no amount of money on earth that will keep him. Money is important, but it isn't everything. Plenty of people give up financially rewarding careers because of psychological pressures or a general lack of fulfilment. In the end, daily discouragement will take its toll no matter how much we might pay.

If it is important for us to give double honour to elders financially, it is similarly important for us to encourage them more generally. Members should tell their elders that they value them. They should be specific in their encouragement. If they are grateful for their preaching, let them know. If their teaching is well-received, tell

---

8 Pond, *Only Servants*, p.153

them. If their pastoral care and general encouragement in the Christian life has been significant, make sure you tell them. This sort of encouragement will keep your elders pressing on. If they cannot see the point of what they are doing, if there seems to be no value in their work – just as with anyone else doing anything else – they will soon give up. Members must let their elders know that what they are doing is valuable, it has purpose and it is bearing fruit. Nothing will encourage your elders more than to see you grow. Nothing will make them want to press on in the ministry more than when they see you listening to the word as it is preached and taught and then responding to it as it changes you. Where you see these things in yourself, where you see them in others, tell your elders. They won't see everything and they are as prone to discouragement as anybody else. But seeing people grow up to maturity in Christ, seeing people shaped by the word, is the entire reason they are in the role. Encourage them by showing them their work has not been in vain.

We need to bear in mind that most pastors do not have a five-day working week. Typically, pastors only get one day off per week. The work of teaching the word, pastoral counselling, setting church vision and organising all manner of things in the church is draining work. Your pastor is human and needs rest. That means, church members can love their pastors well by respecting their day off. If you need some counsel from him, save it for the next day. If you have an emergency on the pastor's day off, take it to another elder. As it happens, the overwhelming majority of pastoral emergencies are really no such thing. Even most big and serious matters – like a marriage falling apart – do not happen overnight. Things may have come to a head, but they have been months or years in the making. Waiting one more day and honouring the need for your leaders to rest will not exacerbate the issue. If you do not want those same issues to be replicated in your pastor's family, he needs to be able and actively encouraged to spend time with his wife and children. He is only in the role of elder because of his approach and relationship to his family (it is an eldership qualification after all). This means they, and not the church membership, are his first priority. The church has the pastor's attention six days of the week. His family frequently feel the burden of his being pulled away or distracted most of the week. We can love and honour both the pastor and his family by properly respecting his day off.

Perhaps most importantly of all, members must pray for their elders. Jesus said, 'you can do nothing without me' (Jn. 15:5). This is true for elders. Apart from Jesus, they have nothing and can do nothing. Elders need their people to pray for them. They minister under the Chief Shepherd, in accordance with his word, by the power of the Holy Spirit at work in them. Of themselves, they are nothing. It is vital, then, that we hold up our leaders in prayer.

Prayer not only does something for our elders, but it does something in us too. It is difficult to hate your elders whilst you are meaningfully praying for their good. We are less minded to criticise our elders when we are actively praying for them. We are more likely to see the good in what they do when our prayers are directed towards them doing good in the church. We are more likely to get something out of their preaching when we are praying that the Lord would speak to us through their preaching. We are more likely to love them when we are praying that God would help us love them and that we would see the ways they are seeking to love us. Prayer is not just a means of changing things in the world, nor of changing how effective our elders might be; it also changes us and our attitudes. Prayer is as important for our elders to receive as it is for us to give. Everybody benefits when there is a spirit of heartfelt, meaningful prayer in the church. 'Happy is the church where the people love the elders and the elders love the people, and they all love the Lord! Watch such a church – good things are bound to happen.'[9]

9 As quoted in Pond, *Only Servants*, p.156

Conclusion

Hardly any book, article or blog post on eldership ends without a rueful 'who is adequate for these things?' I suppose this one should be no different. Being an elder is a daunting task of eternal significance. At times, it seems impossible. Who, apart from Jesus himself, can do it? We should all take the task of eldership seriously and pause to properly understand its weight. But let me end with three brief words of encouragement.

First, let's remember that the task of leading the church to faithfulness is God's work and not ours. Jesus is the Chief Shepherd and we are his under-shepherds. Whilst, yes, elders will be called to give an account before the Lord for how they shepherded the flock (cf. Heb. 13:17), the buck does not ultimately stop with us. Paul says in Philippians 2:13, 'it is God who is working in you both to will and to work according to his good purpose.' What a comfort that is! Jesus is the Chief Shepherd – the buck stops with him! We serve as his under-shepherds and, even then, only as God is working in us. We serve, not in the power of our own might and will, but in the power of God's Spirit at work within us. Amazingly, Paul tells the Ephesians that God 'is able to do above and beyond all that we ask or think according to the power that works in us' (3:20). So even if the task of eldership seems impossible to us, God can do above and beyond what we can even imagine, by his Spirit working in us the works he has called us to do. This means, elder, you can lead the church and you can be up to the task! Not because of your greatness or brilliance, but because of God's Spirit at work in you to this end. Eldership is possible, men are made adequate for it, not in and of themselves, but by God at work in them and through them.

Second, let's remember that if we love Jesus, we will do what he calls us to do. It is my view that if we are qualified to be an elder, and a church is calling us to be an elder, we need very good reasons to say no. I am not saying such reasons never exist, but I am saying those reasons need to be extremely compelling. If we think our elders are at all godly, and our churches at all competent to determine who their leaders should be, don't we need a very compelling reason to suggest they got our calling wrong? If the keys of the kingdom are exercised by the church, and the right to call its own leaders is exercised by the church, do we not need good reason to defy the collective view of the church? Scripture is full of men who were called directly by God yet felt inadequate for the role. Many of them tried to wriggle out of the ministry to which they had been called. Yet, if God equips the people he wants for the tasks he wants them to do, our disposition should be to serve. Remember: whatever reasons you have for not serving (other than being biblically unqualified), somebody else may well have to take up what you are unwilling to do. If we really love the church, and we really love others, we need better reasons than feeling inadequate before we turn down a call to eldership.

Third, 1 Peter 5:4 tells us clearly there is an 'unfading crown of glory' to be gained. The work may be hard, may even seem impossible at times, but those who faithfully shepherd the flock Jesus has entrusted to their care will receive a reward from the Chief Shepherd himself. All the work, all the toil, all the trouble will not be wasted. We don't serve in eldership with a temporal mindset. If we do, we will almost certainly quit. But we can press on knowing that it is God who empowers us to do the work by his Spirit and there is a glorious reward to be gained when we love the Lord Jesus enough to persevere in this great task. When he returns, if we have sought to be faithful to him in the power of the Spirit, we will regret absolutely none of the time we spent in his service. The difficulties will fade away and the trials and conflicts will be but a distant memory as we see Jesus and hear him say to us, 'well done, good and faithful servant.'

Keep pressing on!

Scripture Index

Grace Publications seeks to serve Christ Jesus and his church by producing biblically faithful books that bring the truth of the gospel home to us. Our titles range across church health, Baptist history and doctrine, and Christian living.

Please visit our website to view our full catalogue and to access free articles and media designed to help you grow in your faith.

www.gracepublications.co.uk